ABOUT THE AUTHOR

Anthony Cleary read law at University. After a brief foray into advertising, he decided to return to the law and qualified as a solicitor, later becoming a District Judge. He is now a Circuit Judge, sitting on the Midland Circuit and lives with his wife and son in Warwickshire.

NOBODY COMES

Anthony Cleary

CRUX PUBLISHING

First published in the United Kingdom in 2014
by Crux Publishing

ISBN-13: 978-1-909979-06-2
Also available as an ebook:
eISBN: 978-1-909979-05-5

Requests for permission to reproduce material from this work should be sent
to hello@cruxpublishing.co.uk
www.cruxpublishing.co.uk

To George Dominic

INTRODUCTION

"There are no constraints of the human mind, no walls around the human spirit, no barriers to our progress, save those we ourselves erect."

Ronald Reagan, *State of the Union address*, 06 February 1985

Having been conceived, I guess, around about VE Day, I was born into the 'Baby Boomer' generation. No doubt many others born in the mid 1940s will remember, as I do, when the Berlin Wall went up. I was staying with a young friend with whom I had shared many long hot summer holidays idling our time around his orchard, clucking at his hens and riding our bikes between the geese, laughing as our bells and their honks shouldered out the insect-humming air.

I was a carefree youngster and understood nothing of the significance of the black-and-white images flashing across his father's television. But I recall the deep sense of sadness that fell over the house that morning, as the partition of Europe took on a more sinister shade.

As my generation grew up in selfish introspection, Bill Haley shocked and excited our parents, while we grew our hair to unheard-of lengths, flirted with LSD, and swung our way in, through and out of the Sixties. We had only seen peace, and our families had apparently never had it so good. There might have been occasional interruptions to our feel-good factor – the Cuba missile crisis, devaluation, a winter of discontent, the three-day week – but on the whole, we became accustomed to and rather liked the Gospel According to Mrs Thatcher, market forces, and the ability of the strongest to grab as much capital as possible, believing the wisdom that wealth would trickle down to those below us from our own profligacy.

While our American cousins appeared to be apprehensive of Russian hegemony, we were more curious than scared, and we rather liked the intrigue of the Third Man and then Smiley, as the dastardly secret services of the Communist bloc conspired to overthrow the Western imperialists.

Gradually, in the last quarter of the 20th century, we began to realise that we owed more to life and each other than simply dancing the night away on our little island. Television became an information tool as well as a source of entertainment. Michael Buerk took us to the Horn of Africa and appalled us with scenes of dying children. Bob Geldof channelled our dancing into giving. We learned the meaning of the Third World.

However, we still had no concept of how our neighbours in Europe were living. Millions of people behind the Iron Curtain looked westward, imagining wealth and security and, above all, freedom from totalitarian regimes which ruled them with an iron heel. We chose, however, not to look eastward too carefully, for there was no benefit in it. The Russians, the Warsaw Pact, the East Germans were all objects of at best, intrigue and at worst, fear. Anecdotal evidence persuaded us that protection was needed against our Eastern neighbours, and both television and cinema fiction revealed just how uncomfortable it was to live within those regimes.

When cracks appeared in the edifice, we joined in the general rejoicing – first Poland, and then East Germany, and, of all places, the mighty USSR, revealed an inability to control the groundswell of a popular determination to break out, westward, if not in body, certainly in mind.

And then, a sea change. The closed, even sinister, world surrounding the line of Russian Presidents whom I could remember either from recent history books or from my own lifetime, Lenin, Stalin, Bulganin, Khrushchev, suddenly lurched towards tolerance and reason. President Gorbachev, a man with whom Margaret Thatcher famously proclaimed she could 'do business' took centre stage in Russia. Overnight, and with little apparent opposition from the Kremlin, outlying states of the Soviet Union sought to wriggle free from the Communist yoke. Suddenly, we could not simply look over the Berlin Wall, we could look through it, as students and young people swarmed over it, breaking it down.

The power of television not only recorded but appeared to provoke change throughout the continent. And inevitably, the dissatisfaction of the life endured for so long by the people of Romania welled up; mass meetings developed into revolution, and revolution into assassination. A particularly nasty brand of dictatorship was brought to an end.

But what was left was a damaged country rife with

corruption and with a stagnant economy. And there was more. There were tens of thousands of children, Ceauşescu's children as they became known, who were living in utter squalor.

ONE

"There are things known and things unknown
And in between are the doors."

William Blake, *The Marriage of Howard Hall*, 1757–1827

The Ilyushin seemed to be gliding rather than under power. I looked out of the window as we dropped, silently, towards the ground. Everything seemed to be grey – the high cloud cover, the horizon, and the large, apparently barren, fields below.

We seemed to be entering an empty, even dead, world, without life and without movement. I saw no cattle, no crops, and, indeed, no activity at all. Just bare, dusty fields, with no farm machinery nor even any sign of habitation.

As we dropped lower, I saw the beginnings of a very large airfield and the first signs of life, a line of half a dozen jet aircraft with air force markings, drawn up at the edge of a runway. Their wings glinted as we passed overhead, although I could not, still, detect any sunlight. There was no sign of activity around them but, somehow, their very presence suggested a vaguely menacing alertness.

There seemed to be nothing else, even as we landed. The pilot appeared to nurse the plane down to the ground, so gentle was the contact with the tarmac. I could see nothing out of the window other than the continuous grey runway surface and some grey trees in the distance.

The ground rumbled beneath our wheels, and we slowed, braking in a regular but slowing rhythm.

We taxied into Romania.

TWO

"Life is made up of the most differing, unforeseen,
contradictory, ill assorted things; it is brutal, arbitrary,
disconnected, full of inexplicable, illogical and
contradictory disasters which can only be classified
under the heading of 'Other news in brief'."

Maupassant, *Pierre et Jean*, 1887

January 1990, latitude −34 degrees south, longitude
172 degrees east, the north-western seaboard of
Northland, New Zealand.

Descendants of European settlers, or *Pakeha*, frequently
allow the glorious landscapes of their country to speak for
themselves. Likewise, their Australian neighbours have a
way of telling it how it is. If they want to give a name to
a large river, for example, they choose a name which, to
them, is obvious: 'Big River'. There is a small bird found
in eastern Australia with the most attractive plumage and
charming song. That same bird has a habit of searching for
prey on exposed mud flats, leading to its rather dull but,
one supposes, factually correct name of Mud Skipper. New
Zealand, where I was brought up for my first few years until
my mother decamped to England, makes little effort to

attach colourful or grandiose names to objects which speak quite loudly enough for themselves. The Maori would name features of the landscape in the poetry of their tongue, giving lakes, mountains, and plains an almost mystical quality. Without a written language, their long descriptions have been translated into phonetic, Anglicised versions, which themselves seem to add mystery and rhythm. But where no Maori name existed, the early European visitors, like their Australian cousins, wasted little effort.

1990 was the year of the Commonwealth games in Auckland. I found myself on one glorious midsummer morning standing on Ninety Mile Beach, a mathematically inaccurate name (it is, in fact, closer to fifty miles long) which is quite incapable of doing any justice to the sound and sight of water meeting land in front of me. The most beautiful and unspoiled golden sand stretching as far as the eye could see on a wide, wholly uninterrupted vista, rising gently on my right to an unbroken line of cliffs, and falling away on my left, some seventy metres away, to the roaring breakers of the Tasman Sea. It seemed to go on for ever, both from behind me and ahead of me, fading into what appeared at first glance to be fog or sea mist, but which, on closer inspection, was salt spray thrown tens of metres into the sky by the waves crashing incessantly on to the sand.

And there was no one there.

I could see the occasional footprint – even a hoof print from time to time – but there was no sign of any human life, no habitation, no camper vans, tents or caravans, and no trace of the detritus or litter which reveals the presence of human beings.

Just this beautiful, powerful, warm sea.

Dressed for an early morning run, I simply ran into the waves, exhilarated. My eldest brother had been keen to inform me that the amount of water that would fill the average household fridge would weigh approximately one ton. And fridge after fridge and then more fridges cascaded onto the beach, plucked me up and threw me back each time that I dived, head first, into the breakers.

The heavy artillery shouldered its way over and under me, while the cavalry triumphantly rose and swept forward, chasing the battalions of infantry further and further up the beach, bustling and scrambling for footholds, before rushing back to regroup for the next assault.

And all the time, the noise of this tumult and the drifting salt spray hung over my senses.

Time stood still.

I lay, exhausted but invigorated at the very edge of the waterline, meeting only the advance guard scampering up the beach towards me before retreating, giggling and jostling, back to the next breaker.

As I looked through the spray up at the bright blue sky, I wondered what could get better than that? At that moment, rather selfishly, I considered that I was, after all, in the best of all possible worlds.

***

But, of course, moments like that could not – and indeed should not – last. And I was brought down to earth pretty rapidly that evening when I put a call through to my wife, Carmel, at home in England. She had not joined me in New Zealand because she cannot set foot in an aeroplane, but she was always very supportive of my comparatively infrequent trips back to where I consider to be my homeland, to be with my brothers and my father's family. In this call, however, it was clear, despite the poor connection, that she was unhappy.

"What's the matter?" I said. "Are you all right?"

"Not wonderful. Have you seen the reports coming out of Romania?"

"The *New Zealand Herald* isn't exactly strong on the northern hemisphere," I replied, before biting my tongue at my insensitivity. "Well, no," I spoke more softly, "I haven't."

The *New Zealand Herald* was a newspaper more noted for its charm than its coverage of events on other continents – the reader was treated to a diet of local and parochial snippets. I had not seen television for days, if not weeks. One of the blessings, at least in those days in New Zealand, was the comparative concentration of the broadcast media, both radio and television, on the affairs of the local community and a limited amount of coverage of current affairs in the wider southern hemisphere. Exposure, in England, to three broadsheet newspapers, and both national and international coverage of news on three separate TV channels was a luxury I wasn't sure that I missed.

I explained that I really didn't know what it was that had upset her.

"You remember before you left that we saw that man in charge of Romania being executed with his wife?"

"Yes, sure, it was Ceauşescu and his nasty-looking spouse. It was rather brutal, but I suppose it saved the expense of a show trial."

"That's a horrid thing to say, but that's not the point."

"And the point is?"

I stopped – each time we spoke, we interrupted each other. The typical echo which one had to endure over these thousands of miles meant that we had to adopt what my ex-RNZAF father called the old 'RT" practice, Receive – Transmit, saying one's piece, and then shutting up while the other person replied. One word or even a cough transmitted over the phone would effectively block out anything being sent by the other.

After a pause, she carried on.

"There are these dreadful news flashes coming in from Romania showing thousands of children locked up in orphanages. No one seems to know how they got there, although it's been suggested that it's the fault of the government, or Ceauşescu, and they are in the most dreadful state of repair."

"Who are," I said, trying to be flippant, "the children or the orphanages?"

"You wouldn't say that if you had seen them." She sounded genuinely upset.

"I'm sorry, that was silly of me. What's going on? What have you seen?"

She told me that news teams had had access to what appeared to be orphanages in Romania and had found children in the most dreadful state of neglect, in buildings which were falling down around them.

There appeared to have been a universal cry for help for the country – to provide clothing, food, and even toys for these poor wretches, who appeared, in many instances, to be half-starved.

They were crammed together in the most unpleasant living conditions and were horribly deprived.

Already, tradespeople of every description were on their way to try and carry out repairs to the crumbling buildings in which the children were housed. Trucks with food and clothing – some in convoys, some individually from local church groups and the like – were heading east across Europe in a confused but generous attempt to do something, anything, to address the suffering in the faces of the poor waifs who were caught on camera.

"Well, the sooner you get back here, the better, because you need to see the coverage on UK television of what has been revealed in Romania. It really is quite dreadful. TV cameras have entered a number of orphanages, showing children who have been left to waste away, either through government indifference or lack of money to care for them.

"There are many people going across even now to try and help – painters, decorators, electricians, plumbers, you name it. When you come back, I want you to see what you can do."

"Ah, yes," I replied. "You know that I would be very happy to get stuck in, but you also know that I only have to look at a shelf and it falls down."

My legendary DIY skills had been the butt of many family jokes over the years, and I was not entirely sure what I could do to contribute positively towards any aid endeavour which required skills of plastering, wiring, or painting. Even hammering nails might be a problem.

Nonetheless, I was perfectly happy to return home at the end of the Games and be brought to account, and Carmel seemed marginally reassured when we rang off.

What on earth, I wondered, had been discovered? I had not recalled any particular news item when I left for New Zealand, but obviously things were now being unearthed which demanded international attention. My usual disinclination to read any newspapers on holiday was replaced by a need to access as much current news as I could, and the next day, on my return to Auckland, I got hold of the main broadsheet, and a back issue of *The Times*.

Sure enough, it was reported that things looked pretty bleak and that, as Carmel had said, television crews and reporters had found their way into a number of orphanages, broadcasting footage which revealed buildings in a dreadful state, and children in worse. I knew of the revolution in Romania, which was itself not many months old, and I knew also that President Ceaușescu and his wife had been shot by firing squad. Countries within the Warsaw Pact had, for some time, been shaking off either direct Soviet rule or the governments of puppet dictators. The Iron Curtain still existed, but was itself retreating, and a new dawn, heralded in particular by the demolition of the Berlin Wall, had given all of us, particularly those who had seen the wall being built in the first place, hope for a new Europe and a less anxious life.

Now, however, it seemed that those positive developments were being accompanied by harsh reality. Reports suggested that the poverty, let alone the instability, in countries like Albania, Bulgaria, and Romania appeared to have persuaded those countries that if family income was so meagre that a child or children could not be properly nurtured or fed, then the children should be removed to 'orphanages', notwithstanding that one or even both of the child's parents remained alive. It was taken that the state would provide a basic standard of care and certainly a better one than that which was available to the parents – and it was even imagined that there would be a time when the family's situation would improve, and the child or children could be returned.

But things had, it seemed, got out of hand. Children had been discarded and put into these establishments and simply abandoned. Such was the demand that government ability to provide adequate resources for their children – in terms not only of food, warmth, and adequate buildings, but also in terms of staffing – simply did not exist. If plans had been made, they were not followed.

To Western eyes, the situation appeared appalling and cruel, and, as Carmel had said, a wave of volunteers had already begun to sweep across Europe to see what could be done for the children. Not only were convoys of aid making their way across the continent, but medical staff, sacrificing their own leave and even in many cases, wages, were taking time off to access the orphanages to see what they could contribute toward an increasingly problematic presentation of malnutrition, developmental delay, and disability, both mental and physical.

I was, of course, powerless in New Zealand, but it was not long before I had returned to England, when Carmel gave me more examples of the horrors which had been unearthed during my absence. From what she said, it seemed that our television screens were full of more revelations every day.

Then, only days after I had returned, breakfast television included an interview with a young student doctor who had himself only recently returned from Romania. Carmel and I were riveted by what he had to say. He had been assigned to one of the orphanages and had first-hand knowledge of the conditions in which the children were existing. And there was worse.

"The aid, the comforts, large and small, from blankets to toothpaste – everything that householders back in England are putting together for transmission across to Romania – is being pilfered," he said. "It simply will not get through to the children. Even if the aid gets to the orphanage itself, it is then taken away by the staff, who take it all home.

"While there is no excuse for it, it is simply the case that the economy in Romania is in such a dreadful state that many of the staples which householders in the UK regard as almost a birthright, staples which are so commonplace and which can be easily transmitted by lorry from England to Romania, are simply unavailable anywhere in the country to anyone other than those who can afford to buy goods in 'dollar shops'.

"I beg everyone who is watching this programme," and he looked directly into the camera, "please do not send aid.

It will not get to the children. Instead, we, you, everyone, must move heaven and earth to get the children out of those places."

The interviewers appeared to struggle to find words to say in response to his plea. Either it was wholly unexpected or they were caught up in the emotion of the moment, an emotion which was certainly shared by Carmel and me, for we looked on in stunned silence while this young medic recounted his own experiences.

The programme moved on and I, of course, had to go to work. There was little time to say anything and indeed neither of us knew quite what to say, so troubling was that news item. But one thing was clear. Carmel had made up her mind. Her husband might well be hopeless at DIY, but what we could not provide in terms of skilled labour, we would offer, instead, by way of a loving home.

"I think it would be a good idea if you went over there and brought back a child – perhaps two."

Half-ducking the issue and half in agreement, I had to get to work. "Okay," I replied, before climbing into my car. "Sounds like a plan."

THREE

"Man cannot discover new oceans unless he has the courage to lose sight of the shore."

André Gide, *Les faux-monnayeurs*, 1869–1951

The plane came to a halt, and the engines died. I assumed, in an effort to save energy and gasoline, that the pilot had chosen to turn off every possible drain on his electrics and fuel. The air conditioning shut down, and the cabin lights were switched off.

Almost immediately, the aeroplane became hot and stuffy and increasingly uncomfortable. I peered out of my nearest window to try and get some bearings, but could see nothing except for, in the distance, a line of trees. On the other side of the aisle, my fellow passengers were looking out, but I couldn't see past their shoulders to establish whether or not there were any buildings in sight.

It took about a quarter of an hour for anything to happen. Then I saw two cars pull up next to the aircraft, and from somewhere out of sight, a mobile stairway was produced and put up against the side of the plane. Our door was opened by a flight attendant, but any hope that this would be accompanied by cool, fresh air was dashed when it became clear that one of the reasons that the cabin was so stuffy was that the temperature outside was even more uncomfortably hot.

From the cars, up the stairs and into the aircraft climbed three characters straight out of Central Casting. Broad, Slavic-looking, grim faces, raincoats and homburg hats, they came up the aisle looking from side to side, glaring at each passenger as if to seek out an enemy of the State.

There had been no welcoming message over the intercom that I could identify, and there was certainly no hint of welcome in the faces of these three men as they traversed the aircraft. Apparently satisfied that, at least outwardly, there was no Western spy on board, the three about-turned, descended the stairs and returned to their cars, which drove off.

However, any assumption that this meant that we were now free to disembark was clearly unfounded, since we then waited a further quarter hour without any progress at all, it seemed, being made.

I sat back and thought about our situation. It had been agreed that I should travel to Romania with my mother rather than Carmel, but meeting my mother at Heathrow had been a shock. She was dreadfully overweight. I knew that many heavy smokers who gave up smoking found it difficult to keep control of their weight, but my mother was now in a different league. She was clearly finding it difficult even to walk anywhere at a reasonable pace, and she didn't look particularly happy carrying her one, thankfully small, suitcase.

There was nothing I could say. I was grateful that she had immediately jumped at the chance to come to Romania with me, but I wondered to myself whether she knew what was ahead of us both. I, of course, had no idea, but I doubted that it would be easy and I was immediately concerned that she might not be able to cope.

Language was probably not going to be a major problem – it was already clear from the signs on the plane and from my limited research that French was the second language of most Romanians. I knew my mother was pretty good at languages, and I had spent a summer vacation *en famille* in southern France when I was a teenager, learning to speak the language or, effectively, starve. No, it wasn't communication which troubled me, it was the ability to get around.

We had made ourselves as comfortable as possible on the plane, which, mercifully, was only a little more than half full, and although leg room was extremely cramped, both she and I were able to sit with empty seats on either side of us.

During the flight itself, we had had a foretaste of the deprivation which we were to witness at first hand. It was a small example, but a telling one. The in-flight catering was clearly a resource which Tarom, the state airline, could not afford to purchase outside Romania, and consequently the passengers were treated to the sight of a tea trolley advancing up the aisle bearing a battered metal tea urn. With the cup of tea, assuming one accepted it, the stewardess offered us a piece of stale bread and a small piece of ham. My mother declined it, while I nibbled at the bread and drank the tea.

While we waited on the tarmac, I took a longer look at my mother. She had slept for most of the flight, but had not looked particularly comfortable. I tried to convince myself that the cause was the relatively spartan aircraft and the increasing stuffiness inside the cabin rather than anything more fundamental, but I wasn't convinced.

Finally, as we endured the mounting heat, an ancient single-decker bus wheezed up and pulled to a halt at the aircraft steps, and with apparent reluctance, the flight attendants invited us to move out of the aeroplane.

My mother and I were lucky enough to be close to the front of the cabin, and so we found a place on the bus in the first tranche of passengers to be released from the plane. When it became clear that one bus was not enough, our unhappy fellow travellers had to remain in the cabin while we were taken to the terminal and disgorged to allow the bus to return.

This achingly slow pace gave me an opportunity to survey the terminal before we entered. Towering above us was a rather unpleasant-looking large cube made, it seemed, either of wood or with wood facings and a significant amount of dirty glass. It had all the appearance of one of the worst examples of 60s' brutalism. It did not exude menace – it was simply thoroughly unpleasant.

Eventually, joined by the remaining passengers, we entered the building in a bedraggled crocodile, through the beginnings of the arrivals hall, to collect our luggage. We moved, in single file, past a cubicle which appeared to house some sort of border control. Each of us proffered our passport, and, almost unseen behind the glass partition, an official stamped it, without appearing to take the least interest in its contents.

We moved on, through a small door into a cramped area which was almost devoid of light. I couldn't see any form of carousel, but eventually, an official switched on an elderly angle-poise lamp and pulled the cord of a petrol generator, which struggled into life with something of a clatter. This appeared to power an ancient conveyor belt behind a rubber screen, and slowly, to the sound of a dreadful rattling, suitcases began to push through the screen onto a set of metal rollers which themselves came in a straight line down the centre of the room toward the waiting passengers.

In the gloom, I could make out suitcases, baby-walkers, boxes – the usual detritus from a disembarkation. Each passenger who recovered his or her belongings was given a cursory check by bored-looking Customs officials who, with a piece of chalk, would make a faint mark on whatever possessions were produced to them, after which they and, in due course, we, emerged into the main hall of the terminal.

FOUR

"We learn from experience that not everything which is incredible is untrue."

Cardinal de Retz, *Memoirs*, 1673–76

Carmel and I share a similar characteristic, that of impatience. In many people, that is translated into brisk efficiency. In our case, however, it translates into getting on with things at a rush, without necessarily considering tangential or, indeed, any consequences. From the moment that young doctor appeared on the screen, our minds, our common aim, became fixed, and by unspoken agreement, we were not prepared to tolerate any obstruction.

Initially, we had no plan, but at least we knew that every stage of what we were about to undertake was sequential and that until we had completed one stage, it was pointless proceeding to the next.

We were prepared to take our cues and follow directions from any contact we could find, anyone with experience of Romania and even of bringing a child out. And so, quite fortuitously, it seemed, we had found within a matter of days that an English newspaper, the *Daily Express*, was itself following the fortunes of a young couple who had travelled to

Romania with the declared intention of adopting two babies.

Their story was already provoking considerable interest and was obviously good 'copy', but it was short on detail. Of course, the average reader would not be terribly interested in the nuts and bolts of the expedition, but I needed detail and I needed to know exactly what steps should be undertaken if I was to be successful.

This being before the gloomy days of data protection, the *Daily Express* news desk was prepared to give out the telephone number of the couple, Ian and Paula Marriott, and they, for their part, did not immediately hang up when I made contact.

"It's chaotic," Ian told me. "There is no adoption legislation in place and the government is at sixes and sevens. You have to rely on local government, such as it is, to provide you with the necessary documentation to enable you to get out of the country and back here with a child."

"So, is it right that you have actually managed to bring two children back into the UK?"

"Yes, we have, and we're very relieved that we have managed to rescue them. But if you think that this was just an adventure, and we did it as a knee-jerk reaction, then think again. Adoption is a serious commitment which must not be undertaken lightly."

I wondered if I was going to be treated to a lecture on childcare, and whether I was expected to explain my own motives. However, I bit back on my response and let him carry on.

"I promise you that this isn't a frivolous enquiry. I absolutely agree that this is not a time for adventure; it is a mission partly to rescue and partly to look forward and provide nurture for children who are currently abandoned with no future whatsoever. My wife and I realise that the challenge is probably immense, but the reward will be greater. Not a reward for us, but for the child or children."

I told him that I had already heard of the need for a Home Study report by my own local authority and that I would have to make contact with the local social services office.

"I understand the need for social enquiry reports when adoption is being undertaken either in this country or from abroad, and I can assure you that my wife and I will allow ourselves to be subjected to the necessary scrutiny to satisfy the childcare authorities in this country and, hopefully, in Romania."

That seemed to satisfy Ian, who, it turned out, was more than anxious to help. I immediately regretted my initial but thankfully unspoken reaction to his questions – it became clear as we spoke that he had the best interests of his and the remaining children at heart.

"Okay, this in general terms is what you have to do, and is best described by what we did.

"We travelled to Romania without the faintest idea of where we might find a child. To give us some guidance, we made contact first of all with the Romanian embassy in London and they, for their part, appeared willing to give us a list of orphanages which might be prepared to co-operate with us.

"For the privilege of entering the country and following up our enquiries we had to pay some sort of visa fee, which seemed pretty pointless and designed only to produce some foreign exchange.

"In fact, there's a travel agent in Hertfordshire, trading as Friendly Travel, a chap called Harry McCormick, who's prepared to offer special deals to couples travelling to and from Romania on these adoption missions."

He gave me the address and phone number of the agent, and went on:

"When you get there, you must decide on the area which you wish to investigate and then, as we discovered, it would be a good idea to find yourself a taxi driver who can act as guide and interpreter. That is exactly what we did, and we spent a day moving between orphanages, seeking to identify the babies whom we could bring back to the UK."

"When you have found the babies, you need the consent of the mother to the removal and adoption of the children. Then you need the authority of the local mayor, and once you have that, you get hold of the President, who signs it off, and when that's been done you can return to the United Kingdom, provided you have entry clearance from the British consulate."

I was writing furiously as he described this remarkable process. The lack of formality seemed more than a little surprising and fraught with snares. But I was assured that the process was actually as simple as it sounded. And the mayor and most of officialdom, according to Ian, were particularly amenable to staples which were only found with great difficulty in Romania – vodka and American cigarettes.

There was evidently no formal procedure and it was, he said, a usually pretty straightforward task to find the

mother, obtain her consent, and then, having obtained
the necessary documentation from the mayor, make one's
way to the President in Bucharest, produce the documents
to the British embassy and obtain clearance to bring the
children back into the United Kingdom.

"And that's it?"

"Well," he said, "it worked for us and it should still
work for you. So, the best of luck."

And that was it. He promised to write to me with all that
he had told me – and I for my part now had a scattering
of scribbled notes taken during our conversation. I hung
up the telephone in a pretty bewildered state. Was it really
possible to extract a baby from an orphanage, find and
effectively bribe an official, and then, with the approval of
the President and, after him, the British embassy, simply
load the child onto an aeroplane and end up back home
in the UK?

Stranger things have happened, I supposed, and there
on the pages of the *Daily Express*, I could see a delighted
young couple with two babies who had at one stage shared
an open suitcase on the trip back to the UK, looking not
only none the worse for the experience, but very much the
better for it.

So, more things to do. Contact the Romanian embassy;
badger my local authority to progress a report on our
circumstances at home; identify possible areas to pursue in
Romania; establish just how I could travel, investigate and
return and complete the trip without Carmel.

This last issue was likely to be something of a problem.
I was a Registrar, a judicial post in the County Court,

employed by the government. I was to discover that my line manager, Robin Holmes, the Courts Administrator, was remarkably sympathetic to my need to take time off, but Carmel was self-employed, working virtually single-handed in her own clothing boutique in Leamington Spa. The clothing trade had not been particularly buoyant for some time, and relied, season by season, on maintaining sales before the stock became unsaleable, as 'dead stock'. Customers at her end of the market were extraordinarily fickle. Each season (for the purpose of buying, that is,) lasted only a number of weeks rather than months, and it didn't take very much, either in terms of weather or economic decline, for sales to fail at a crucial time, leaving the retailer no choice but to discount heavily in a desperate attempt to remove stock from the shelves.

Throughout the existence of her shop, Carmel, like an enormous number of small independent retailers, had to remain at the helm, hands on, with a keen eye to her business overdraft, making visits to London to purchase the following season's stock from a host of independent labels. If she didn't, and given that we both would have to be away from the UK for a good number of weeks, there was little doubt that her business would fail.

Added to that, she couldn't fly. And if she and I were to travel to Romania either by road or train, it was clear that each journey would take two or even three days. I had picked up a complicated-looking volume of European train timetables at our local main train station and established that the rail link to Bucharest from England followed the route of, or even was, the original Orient Express, although the timetable suggested that it was very much a shadow of the romantic transportation described by Agatha Christie. Indeed, it halved in size somewhere along the route, one set of coaches going off in one direction, the other continuing on towards the east.

This was to be no Wagon-lits romance. It was not, as I had protested to Ian Marriott on the telephone, an adventure. It was a mission and it had to be undertaken as efficiently as possible, which meant, in particular, speed, and if I were to find one or even two babies, nursing them on a two- or three-day rail trip would be extremely difficult.

Of course, I did not know the half of it.

But what I did know was that Carmel could not accompany me and I would have to make the trip with someone else. My immediate thoughts turned to my mother – not a woman with the greatest maternal instinct and one who had effectively left much, if not all, of my care to surrogate foster parents and boarding schools while she, for her part, pursued a lifestyle which was not suited at all to either matrimony or child rearing. In her sometimes chaotic travel through life, she had married no less than four times. I was her firstborn, and Lucy, my half-sister, was born to my mother's marriage to my second stepfather. Lucy herself had been left mainly to fend for herself, and although, for a good part of her younger life, she had had to share a home with her mother, it was an unhappy and difficult experience.

But my mother had many attributes, some quite surprising. In my late teens, I recall that she was an assistant governor at Holloway prison in London. Later, she became the first woman to be appointed an assistant governor at a male prison, in Maidstone. She did not stop there and was sent by the Home Office to assist in or, as far as I knew, even run, the women's prison in Kowloon, Hong Kong. In between her third and fourth marriages, she had bought a tiny apartment on a Greek island, and would drive from London, through Europe and into Greece in her battered Austin Allegro without any thought of danger or mechanical breakdown.

I remembered that, when I was about ten, she obtained a pilot's licence, and although I never saw her at the controls of an aeroplane, she had admitted to me that on her maiden solo flight she ran out of fuel and had to crash land, to the delight of the local press, which published a picture of her Tigermoth nose-down in a country ditch.

She had a remarkable brain – she played bridge for Sussex and, indeed, her second husband was also a county player. So also did she have an extraordinary gift for languages. Her second husband was an Israeli, and her third, although not Israeli, was Jewish, and whether for the hell of it or not, I do not know, she learned Hebrew. When appointed to the prison in Kowloon, she learned Cantonese.

Above all, she loved to travel and she loved a challenge.

I had not seen her for ages. After I left university, I had found my own accommodation in a garret in London, while she embarked on her remarkable career changes, moving between partners, some of whom she married, with a rapidity which matched her undeniable speed of thought. Her fourth husband, Freddie North, whom I had met some years before, was an international bridge player and author, with an enormous reputation among the bridge-playing fraternity, but I had only seen the two of them together once since their marriage – the third such ceremony to which I had not been invited.

I could think of nobody else, and so, with some trepidation, I telephoned her.

"Darling," she exclaimed breathily – I imagined I could hear her exhaling streams of cigarette smoke, although I knew very well that she had, remarkably, given up a 50-a-day habit at a stroke some years ago – "how exciting. Of course I will go with you."

Naturally, I was grateful. I gave her the basics and told her that I would be in touch.

What I did not bargain for was her state of health.

FIVE

"The most absurd and the most rash hopes have
sometimes been the cause of extraordinary success."

Vauvenargues, *Reflections and Maxims*, 1746

Next step, a home study report. Ian had told
me to make contact with the Department of
Health rather than the Home Office, and he
explained that written guidance had just been published,
setting out the steps to be taken, with a heavy emphasis
on what should not be done. The home study, as I already
suspected, was perhaps the most crucial document,
which both the Romanian authorities (presumably the
orphanage or maybe the mayor, or even the President)
and the department would need. Oddly, I discovered
that the guidance suggested that the report should not
be sought until after a child had been identified, which
meant a period of uncertainty and delay which could,
I imagined, take months. It seemed to me that it was
important to deal with this fundamental building block
of the whole endeavour right at the start. If there was
to be any problem, it didn't seem sensible to leave that
unaddressed let alone unidentified until after a child had

been found but left behind, while paperwork was being assembled at heaven knows what pace.

And I knew that in the eyes of social workers, I was not young. I was 44 and Carmel a year younger, and no matter that I was active, both in the squash court and on the hockey pitch, I gathered that miles on the clock mattered rather more than good mechanical condition to some local authorities.

So I put my hand to the word processor and sent off a letter to my local social services office. The reply was short and to the point. Home studies were not being undertaken by this local authority and probably not by others, either. Resources, slim as they were, were concentrating upon the needs of children within the county, and therefore, unfortunately, no assistance would be provided to me.

On reflection, that might well have been a reasonable standpoint, but in my heightened state, I was not prepared to accept no for an answer, and so I pressed the point. I telephoned the author of the reply.

"Can you tell me whether I'm right in believing that you actually have a statutory duty to carry out a home study report?"

"No, I don't think we do," she replied. "And even if there was such an obligation, it would have to be balanced against our duties to the children within the county."

"But children come into the county from all directions," I said, "both home and abroad, and you are obliged, of course, to carry out your duties under the Children Act in respect of all, and not just those whom you choose."

That sounded far more unpleasant than I meant it to

be, but before I could mend the fence that I had started to trample down, my contact retorted, "No matter what you say, you can't tell me how this authority should manage its obligations to our families."

Clearly I was going to get nowhere but I had a last throw. "Look," I said, "You and I are not going to agree on whether you should or should not devote resources to this particular task, but I'm going to have to ask you to refer the case to the Director of Social Services. If he maintains the same view that you have described, then I propose to take the matter further, to the department in London, and if necessary to the Secretary of State."

"Well," she said, "you'll have to put that in writing, and until you do and the Director takes a different view, I'm afraid that we can't help you further."

Thank goodness, I thought to myself, she didn't end the conversation with 'have a nice day'.

By this time, I had built up a head of steam, and I was not prepared to let the matter grind to a halt. In reserve, I had read somewhere that it might be possible to obtain the services of an independent social worker for the preparation of such a report, but as a matter of logic, I wondered whether that would satisfy the British government, let alone the Romanian authorities, given that payment to an independent social worker to compose such a report would be unlikely to produce a negative outcome. At least a local authority social worker would, I took it, be entirely objective and, if appropriate, would say loud and clear if parents could not pass muster. And, of course, the local authority adoption panel would itself be cautious about approving adoptive parents where the documentation before it had been prepared by an expert in his or her field, but an expert in the pay of the proposed adopters.

So the next day, 22 May 1990, I sat down and prepared a letter to the Minister of State for the Department of Health and Social Security, the Right Honourable Virginia Bottomley MP.

I was past caring whether my letter would be greeted with enthusiasm, or indeed if I were to be labelled as some sort of vexatious applicant. Frankly, I doubted that Mrs Bottomley would herself even read the letter, and even if she did, would take a personal interest in my individual problem. What was important, however, was that someone in authority in my local area might not be prepared to take the risk of criticism from London.

And while I waited for the outcome, there were more things to do.

First, Ian Marriott had set out a list of papers which I had to prepare in support of the home study report, and I noted them down in what was to become my travelling dossier:

- a letter from my mortgagee, confirming satisfactory conduct of our home loan;
- confirmation from our accountant of our income and solvency;
- photographs of our home;
- a medical report on each of us;
- references;
- confirmation by a lawyer that British law enabled us to adopt a foreign-born child in the UK;

- a 'Home Office letter' outlining the steps from adoption to approval to entry clearance.

This dossier had then to be notarised in England and then translated into Romanian. He told me of a translator in Bucharest, Lily, who would undertake a translation at half the cost and three times the speed of anyone in the UK. Meanwhile, it had to be 'certified' by the Romanian embassy in London – quite what that entailed escaped me, but, as Ian and I both suspected, it seemed to be a useful, if modest, source of hard currency for the Romanian authorities.

As Ian Marriott told me, "They only accept cash."

While preparing all this, I had to make contact with the Romanian embassy. Again, this was a letter, designed along the general lines described by the Marriotts. I was, they said, to indicate quite openly that I wanted to offer a home to a child or children in an orphanage in Romania and I needed permission to enter the country and an indication of whether or not I could rely on the co-operation of the authorities.

The letter in reply was surprisingly swift, and set out a number of minor stipulations, fees, and an indication of where children could be found. It was the latter disclosure which was the most depressing, for the letter included page after page of addresses, both in town and country, where children were being accommodated. I imagined that these addresses were those which the Romanian government was prepared to reveal, being, I assumed, the least unpleasant of the bunch. Ian had cautioned me that there were far more, but even reading through the enclosures revealed tens of thousands of children, scattered around the country, in the establishments which I knew had only been glimpsed in the television news broadcasts, and which had so distressed not only me but the majority of the British public.

At least I had some certainty. I knew where to go, in London, for my first port of call, I knew what to say, and I knew what to pay. I knew that I would not be challenged about my destination and that the embassy would simply leave it to me to decide where to go. The list which I had composed with Ian's help still required a number of formalities which were not difficult to overcome. My main problem remained: the absence of a home study report.

Then, a week later, the caravan lurched forward. A letter from my local authority, dated 25 May, written three days after my letter to the Secretary of State had arrived in London.

> *"I understand that Mrs Maudsley had communicated to you Warwickshire's policy on adoptions.*
>
> *I am writing to inform you that the Association of Directors of Social Services have very recently issued new advice, which questions this policy. Essentially it does encourage Local Authorities to undertake Home Studies on children from Romanian Orphanages.*
>
> *I will ask Mrs Maudsley to contact you as soon as possible after the Bank Holiday."*

I mouthed a silent 'thank you'. But there was no time to sit back in satisfaction, for the second task which I had set myself was to attempt to find someone who had wider experience of Romania and of the problems we might face. Might I even find a contact who would be of assistance?

Fortune took a hand. The Baptist church in Kenilworth was advertising for clothing and basics of every kind to load up in a regular shuttle service run by the local pastor, Graham Prestridge, who was arranging trips in and out of Romania with, effectively, emergency supplies. With some trepidation, I phoned him and introduced myself.

His response was immediate and charming, but pessimistic.

"I appreciate your motives and how you feel, but you'll not receive any co-operation in Romania itself. The Romanians don't care for their children being removed."

"I don't understand," I replied. "Don't they understand that the children are literally living in a sewer, and that it is vital to remove them?"

"Yes, I think they do."

"Can they remove them, themselves?"

"No," he conceded, "they can't."

"So why on earth do they resent or object to offers from abroad to take the children into loving and supporting homes?"

"I can only imagine that they are anxious about the children losing their birthright."

"But, in heaven's name, their birthright is a pretty long second behind their first right to the unquestioning and loving care of a family which will nurture them into adulthood, when they can, themselves, choose whether or not they wish to examine or fulfil what is rather loosely called their birthright." I marvelled at my apparent pomposity.

Fortunately, the Reverend Prestridge was not troubled by it. "You may be right, and you and I could discuss this and even argue it for hours to come without a satisfactory conclusion. The problem is that the Romanian mind-set is not one which is, at least at the moment, amenable to persuasion that there is a better alternative to leaving the children where they are.

"There are charities out there, both from this country and others, who are desperately trying to extract the children into local hostels or into foster care. The government is not impeding them…"

"I bet it isn't," I muttered.

"… But the task is huge, and it is little more than a drop in the ocean."

"So why on earth are we standing by and allowing this to happen?"

I realised almost as I finished the question just how stupid it was. It was, I suppose, simply an indication of my frustration, but I knew that that alone would get me nowhere. What I needed was to establish whether or not Graham had any contact whom he might suggest I should follow up.

He was extremely reticent. To be fair, he was very probably anxious not to compromise his own attempts to establish some sort of aid route into the country.

"I'll think about it," he said. "I'm travelling to Romania with the next vanload next week, and I should be back in 10 days' time. I hope I'll be able to give you a more constructive answer then."

I realised that I could not really ask for more, and, of course, I knew both that he was himself offering a lifeline to Romania and that he was also being extremely reasonable in our discussions. So I put a lid on my impatience and thanked him as cordially as I could and promised that I would make contact once more on his return. I wished him well for his next endeavour, and underlined my good wishes with the promise of a box of provisions.

Over that weekend, Carmel and I put together a box of soap, toothpaste, T-shirts, socks and household bits and pieces which we reckoned would fit the bill, and I delivered it to the Baptist church for the next convoy. As I did so, I wondered if and when I might follow the box to that unhappy place.

***

I would have to wait for the next 10 days, I realised, before establishing whether or not contact could be made with some sort of support in Romania. But, meanwhile, we received the promised phone call from Mrs Maudsley of the local authority.

"As you know, the Director of Social Services has considered your case and has decided that he will put aside resources so that you may have a home study report prepared for your proposed adoption."

"That is remarkably good news and extremely kind of him," I said.

"He would rather that you didn't write to the department in London, since he has taken this decision on his own initiative."

"Ah," I said. "I have in fact written already and I'm extremely grateful to the Director and I will ensure that if I receive a reply from London, the department is made aware of the local authority's willingness to help. Anyway, what now?"

"Well," said Mrs Maudsley, "the requirement is that we come to your home, carry out interviews with you and your wife and look into your background, check references and prepare a report. If the report is positive, we put it before the adoption panel. You'll appreciate that the investigation that we must undertake is quite intensive."

"I quite understand that and I can promise you that my wife and I will co-operate fully. When do we start?"

To my surprise, I was promised an immediate start, and our first appointment was made there and then.

"This would normally take about eight weeks but we understand your wish to move on as swiftly as possible, given the reports of the state of the children in Romania, and we will endeavour therefore to wrap it all up for you in six weeks. Then we have to wait for the decision of the adoption panel, which can take anything up to another two months to reach a conclusion, simply because of the queue of applications for consideration by the panel which doesn't meet every day of the week."

I avoided voicing my immediate sense of disappointment, realising that steps had to be taken and protocols followed, and that these things could not be done overnight. If we were to succeed in speeding anything up, it would have to be by co-operating fully with the social work team rather than complaining every step of the way.

The important and encouraging thing was that we now appeared to be making progress.

And then, at the promised time, 10 days later, Graham Prestridge made contact.

"I'm going to give you some names," he said. "It is important that you keep my name out of it, because I don't want them to feel that I have betrayed them, and I know that they do not really want to be involved in what Romanians consider to be against rather than in the interests of their children."

He went on, "Let us meet and I will give you a name and a phone number. Then, it's up to you."

Barely able to contain myself, I agreed to get together with him.

Hours later, eager to obtain as much information but remembering to restrain myself, I listened as he told me of the contact whom I might approach.

First, he had heard of a government official and his wife in Romania who had adopted two children themselves. The husband was, it seemed, a clinician in a position of authority for the region around Bacau, in the east of the country, close to the Iron Curtain. He had responsibility for the oversight of three orphanages. He apparently spoke perfect English.

In that same city, there was an English nurse, undertaking some form of liaison between that official, the orphanages and visiting volunteers. She would probably know very much better than anybody what was going on on the ground and where I might undertake my enquiries first.

Finally, I was given the name and phone number of Mary Gibson, the personal assistant of the chief executive of a nascent charity, the Romanian Orphanage Trust, working out of an office in central London. She would be, I was told, the least anxious to be identified, but might well, nonetheless, be prepared to give me some contact details which I could follow up in Romania.

"I'm sorry to bang on about this," he said, "but I really must ask you to respect my wish that you keep everything you hear from me entirely confidential. Of course, you may use the details I have given you, but I really don't want to be identified as the source of this information. I'm sure you understand that I want to be able to move the aid convoy in and out of Romania without losing the trust of my own contacts."

What a curious and depressing overview, I thought. I couldn't wholly grasp the need for caution, and I still couldn't understand why it might be that Romanians could have any doubt about the endeavours of those who desperately wanted to help the children.

"Bear in mind that your motives, and the motives of many others, are entirely Christian and based on the needs of the children. There are others, however, whose motives are sinister – those who have taken children and trafficked them for the most dreadful purposes."

In my innocence and in my desire for speed, I'd never thought about that, and I had given no thought at all to the sordid and unpleasant behaviour of those who would prey on children and take every opportunity to get hold of a baby or an infant for their own appalling and criminal ends.

At least, I hoped, a properly authenticated home study report would prove something of a barrier to criminals and a reassurance to the authorities. Graham agreed, but pretty obviously without great enthusiasm. We shook hands and he wished me well.

SIX

"The secret of getting ahead is getting started."

Mark Twain, 1835–1910

I rang the number that Graham had given me. The voice that answered was so full of exhaustion that, initially, I was lost for words. Eventually, however, I established that I was speaking to Mary Gibson and I told her that I had been given her name by a relief worker, and I knew that she was a key figure in the establishment of the Romanian Orphanage Trust.

"I'm planning a trip to Romania, and I want to know if I can be of any help by taking particular supplies. Provided, of course, I can carry them."

"Well," she answered, "we do have nurses working in Bucharest and they have told us that they simply don't have enough supplies of Hibiscrub, E45 cream and Pholcodine linctus."

I confessed that I had only ever heard of the cream and certainly not the other two.

"The Hibiscrub is an antibacterial wash, and the linctus is desperately needed, because virtually all the children have got upper respiratory tract infections."

"And there's another thing," she continued. "Many of the children, if any of them, have never seen a paddling pool. If you can take over a portable swimming pool, that would be marvellous."

That sounded a bit industrial to me, and I wondered how I could possibly carry a swimming pool.

"Don't worry. You'll be able to find just the job at Argos, and, believe me, these tiny children really could do with a splash about."

"OK, I'll do all that, but I need you to identify the nurses for me so that I can take the stuff to them."

"The ones I'm particularly thinking of are being put up at a hotel in the centre of Bucharest called the Hotel Lido. The government pays for their board and lodging, and they give their time free in exchange."

"I'll deliver the things you've listed for me, but in exchange, I would very much appreciate some information."

I sensed a change on the other end of the line, but I ploughed on.

"My wife and I are planning to rescue one or even two children, and that's the purpose of my visit. I gather that you do have a contact over there, a Romanian official, who has adopted two children of his own and I really would appreciate it if you would give me his name and address."

She was not as reluctant as I had feared, possibly out of tiredness, and she gave me the name of a Doctor Sadovici. Yes, she said, he was not only a paediatrician, but was, as I had been told, a clinician in some sort of government post with responsibility for three orphanages in the Bacau region. And if I was to travel to Bacau she also gave me the name of the English nurse who was acting in some form of liaison capacity and was herself being accommodated in a hotel apartment there.

I thanked her, and promised, again, that I would ensure that the needed supplies, as much as I could carry, would be delivered to the nurses in Bucharest.

As I put the phone down, I felt a surge of optimism. I could not think of a better contact, and I imagined that the path ahead of me was straightening out.

I could not have been more wrong.

SEVEN

"It is not so much our friends' help that helps us as the confident knowledge that they will help us."

Epicurus, 3rd century BC

I sat opposite our GP, David Rapley.

"Morning, David."

"Hi, Tony – to what do I owe the pleasure?"

"I'm going to adopt a Romanian orphan."

He sat up. "Really?"

Thank goodness he didn't start on the 'is that a good idea?' mantra.

"Well, two if I can. Once the home study is completed – and you'll probably find that a social worker will be asking questions about our health for a medical report – I'll not be delaying any further and I'll be getting on a flight."

"So, how can I help?"

"I need some advice – what do I look for? What should I avoid? Are there particular signs which will alert me to things which would signal disabilities or …" I tailed off. I knew so little and hadn't really got a clue what questions I should ask, but visiting the surgery had seemed a reasonable idea at the time.

"Hmm," said David. "I know as much and as little as you do about the conditions over there. Medical care seems pretty sparse and there can be any number of problems facing the children. I suppose that they face malnutrition, developmental delay, and even Aids. The best I can do, given that you will probably be unable to have any clinician on hand to give you the all-clear, is suggest that you aim for a child who is about 12–18 months old.

"By that age you will be able to detect whether the child has started to pick up any sort of speech – but the child's ability to test and use language won't have been so concentrated to prevent him or her quickly understanding English.

"The child should by then be able to walk without help, and you'll be able to identify his gross motor skills without any great difficulty.

"Aids tests are notoriously unreliable with children of that sort of age, but if you have any doubts at all you should try and get to a hospital for a check. Apart from that, you're on your own.

"Just make sure that as soon as you get back to the UK, you arrange to bring the child – or children – here for an immediate check-up."

And that was it. He wished me good luck, we shook hands, and I left the surgery. His advice seemed sensible enough.

Looking back, it showed just how little either of us knew what was ahead.

EIGHT

"The best way out is always through."

Robert Frost, 'A Servant to Servants', 1914

As the home study report progressed, I prepared the dossier, contacting the bank, the accountant, and our referees as I did so. On my way to work, I called in at a large branch of Boots the chemist close by the main train station.

"I shall be travelling to Romania in the course of the next few weeks and I have been asked to take some supplies with me. I'll be travelling by air, and I can only take as much as I can carry, but I would very much appreciate it if you could let me have commercial-sized supplies of E45 cream, and, if it is available without prescription, Pholcodine linctus."

"I can get both," said the manager.

"And what about Hibiscrub?"

"Yes, I can get that for you too."

"How much do I need to buy to get a discount from you?"

"I reckon, since you're taking these to Romania, to the orphanages, that I can let you have all of it at wholesale rates."

"That's really kind," I said. "Can you get me enough to fill a decent-sized rucksack?"

He said he certainly could, but that I had better watch out, because none of it was lightweight. I reassured him that that was the least of my problems, and we arranged for me to pick up the supplies in the following week.

I then paid a visit to Argos.

"Do you have portable swimming pools?" I asked the bemused-looking assistant.

"Well, yes. At least, we have large paddling pools."

"And do they fold up?"

"Sure do. They're made of reinforced plastic, with lightweight metal struts, and they all fit into a box which is easy to carry."

I decided to take three, two for Romania and one to keep at home, in the hope that the child or children whom we brought in to England would delight in splashing about in our back garden.

Then I visited the army surplus store to get hold of a roomy but lightweight rucksack. I wasn't too bothered about style, just space, and I found just the thing – a roomy main compartment, with a number of side pockets, both internal and external, with robust-looking straps and a comfortable harness.

Back at home, I turned my attention to the preparation of a letter of introduction to Dr Sadovici. I wanted to be sure that I could give him proper warning of my arrival, and reassure him as to my intentions, so I spent some time preparing an appropriate description both of me and Carmel and of our home and explaining our motives. Mary Gibson had said that he spoke English but I thought it would be wise to have the letter translated into

Romanian, and after a little research in the legal press, I found a translator in London to whom I sent my offering. It was returned within a week and I decided that it would be a good idea to send it to the nurse in Bacau who was, as Mary Gibson had told me, some sort of liaison person.

Things were beginning to pick up speed. Mrs Maudsley was as good as her word, and prepared her report remarkably quickly after carrying out interviews with both of us and our referees and inspecting our house from top to bottom. She pronounced herself satisfied and assured us that the application would go before the adoption panel far more quickly than she had at first said.

In fact, the whole process took a little less than six weeks, and by early July, with her reassurance that we were likely to get the go-ahead, I was able to contact both the travel agent and my mother and arrange a flight for me and my mother from London to Bucharest on 15 July 1990. Friendly Travel would meet us at Heathrow and give us the tickets and our hotel coupons.

Three days before departure, after Margaret Maudsley had formally confirmed that the adoption panel had approved my request to adopt two Romanian children, I travelled to London, to the Romanian embassy, clutching my dossier with sufficient cash to hand over in exchange for the necessary entry permits.

The embassy itself was an unremarkable building on an extremely expensive piece of London real estate, close, I gathered, to Millionaires' Row. It was immediately identifiable from a distance, with a large Romanian flag hanging from a stanchion fixed to a balcony on the first floor. In the middle of the flag, where hitherto there had been a large circle on which some sort of socialist regalia was emblazoned, there was now a large hole. The effect was rather curious. Six months or so had passed since the socialist regime had been toppled. Why, I wondered, was it still necessary to display the flag in this way?

There was no immediate answer, but, of course, my task was not to examine the political fortunes of Romania or the progress of democracy, but to complete this stage of my journey and so, when a gloomy-looking retainer opened the embassy door to me and told me to wait in a side room, I patiently waited to be called into an office where an equally gloomy but, I suspected, rather more senior member of staff set about stamping the front and back of my dossier, including my and Carmel's birth certificates and our marriage certificate, for which he asked me for the sum of £50. Cash.

I was not entirely sure of the effect of the stamps and the signatures – they appeared to do nothing more than confirm what was clear already – that the document had been notarised and carried the seal of an English Notary Public to that effect and that the London embassy had been paid fifty pounds for the privilege of adding its own stamp, but the official reassured me that I needed nothing more, and that there would be no difficulty entering Romania, for which an advance visa was no longer required; a time-limited visa would be endorsed on my passport upon entry.

There was no more to be said. He didn't ask the purpose of my visit, and it seemed pointless my trying to engage him in conversation. But at least, now, everything seemed in place. I made a quick phone call to my mother to confirm that we would meet at Heathrow, and I returned home to pack everything ready for my expedition.

And on the morning of 15 July, I took a train to London.

NINE

"The nether sky opens, and Europe is disclosed as a prone and emaciated figure, the Alps shaping like a backbone, and the branching mountain-chains like ribs, the peninsular plateau of Spain forming a head. Broad and lengthy lowlands stretch from the north of France across Russia like a grey green-garment hemmed by the Ural Mountains and the glistening Arctic Ocean. The point of view then sinks downwards through space, and draws near to the surface of the perturbed countries, where the peoples, distressed by events which they did not cause, are seen writhing, crawling, heaving, and vibrating in their various cities and nationalities."

Thomas Hardy, *The Dynasts*, 1840–1928

I picked up my rucksack and our two suitcases, wondering if there might be any attempt by Customs to look into our luggage, and what, if I was challenged, would be made of my various supplies – swimming pools from Argos, medical supplies from Boots the chemist, and cigarettes by Kent to name but a few – but I need not have worried. The Customs officers, in their crumpled uniforms, stood huddled together, smoking, showing only the faintest interest in what was going on at the end of the line.

My mother and I moved on to the arrivals hall without the greatest confidence, assuming that those ahead of us knew where they were going, forming a loose line with our fellow passengers. There were none of the multilingual signs that were a customary sight in most airports which I had ever visited and, more by luck than judgement, we found our way to a minibus which appeared to be doing service as some sort of airport shuttle. Our fellow travellers looked as bewildered as we must have done, but about a dozen of us who had either not been met or had not secured taxis climbed into the bus, ushered by two young men who seemed eager to take us on our way into the city, which turned out to be some sixteen or so kilometres away.

I stuttered the name of our hotel to one of them. He responded breezily, in broken English, that there was no problem, and they would be calling there on the way.

Once we got under way, the young man who was not driving took the opportunity to address his passengers, many of whom appeared to be, or at least to speak, English, seeking to persuade us all, with a mixture of charm and something uncomfortably close to begging, to exchange dollars for Romanian currency.

"You will only get about 100 lei for your dollar," he explained, "and I can give you a far better rate. Anyway, you are not just doing yourselves a favour but you are helping us, because we really do need foreign currency very badly indeed."

It was difficult to resist him. I knew very well that the official exchange rate was pitifully small, since Graham Prestridge had spoken of just 50 lei to the dollar, and whereas I also knew that it was quite likely that the rate he was offering was itself not the best black-market rate, I could see no harm in exchanging a few dollars for the wedges of notes which he produced from his plastic case.

Ten US dollars produced about three thousand lei, which I had to stuff into various pockets of my jacket as we travelled through the heat of the afternoon into Bucharest. There was nothing to see from our windows and very little traffic on what appeared to be one of the few dual carriageways that we were to encounter during our visit.

Our driver knew where he was heading, and after half an hour, he pulled up at the hotel which had been reserved for us by Friendly Travel. We were the only two passengers to disembark.

From the outside, Hotel Parc was unremarkable; a modern, square block, which seemed to be some six or so stories high, with a substantial parking area in front of it, made up primarily of a long wide drive to the front, divided by a long row of sorry-looking trees, populated in the main by a scattering of heavy-goods vehicles and some private cars.

The architectural style appeared to be similar to the 'modern brutalist' style which I had first seen at the airport, resembling a sort of upended cement cube, while inside there was an overwhelming sense of vertical and horizontal lines, with little consideration given to comfort. Opposite the main entrance was a long reception desk, backed up against the rear wall, extending to the whole width of the vestibule. To my surprise, however, the young receptionist who greeted us spoke extremely good English. He introduced himself as Mircea and looked at our reservation coupons. He said they were satisfactory and that they entitled us, it seemed, to a room on the second floor.

He apologised, saying that the lift was not working, but he obviously assumed that we could take our luggage up the stairs ourselves, for there was no hint of assistance. However, the task was not beyond me, given that we had travelled from London without too much difficulty. The heaviest burden, of course, was the rucksack full of the supplies which I had brought with me but which I was able to sling over my shoulders while we mounted the stairs.

There were two stairwells, one to the side, flanking the non-functioning lift and one ahead. The side stairs were partially blocked by a ragged-looking curtain behind which I could make out a bare light bulb and a suggestion of some long-abandoned repair works. We were able to negotiate the main stairwell and found our way to the room, which appeared to have all the basic amenities – even a television set of uncertain vintage which, on being switched on, produced only one channel, with a wavering picture in black and white.

There was a bathroom, en suite, required by our travel coupon, and, I was to discover, as was commonplace in Romania, there was no plug, either in the bath or in the basin. There was a threadbare towel but no soap. But these were minor matters. We had arrived, and had what appeared to be a basically comfortable room.

And I had work to do. My first task was to make my way to the British embassy and so I suggested to my mother, who looked ready for a lie-down, that I should go there, and hopefully get back in time for tea – although quite what 'tea' would turn out to be remained an open question.

Anyway, free of our luggage, and happy to stretch my legs, I secured a small map of the immediate area from Mircea – in reality, little more than a sketch plan on the back of our little room voucher – and set off for the centre.

***

This was the first part of my planned itinerary. I remembered that Ian Marriott had directed me, "On arrival in Bucharest, go to the British embassy," and I walked straight ahead, obeying the little map in my hand, following something of a major thoroughfare which effectively bisected the city. Where I had set out, there seemed to be a substantial park area, Parcul Nerastrau, with a smaller park, Teneretului, at the other end of the city, and between the two, my route took me from Piata Scinteii through Piata Victoriei and then on to Bul Magheru, part way along this obviously main tributary.

The walk to the city centre began pleasantly enough. Passing from one large square at the head of a wide avenue, 'Kiseleff', which I imagined to be of German derivation, I came by some sort of triumphal arch, then on to another avenue, Ipatescu, which was plainly Romanian. I walked on for what I guessed to be three or four miles before it became clear that I was approaching the centre of the city.

I noticed, as I walked, that a good number of pedestrians would stand in the road, attempting to flag down cars. Initially, I wondered what on earth they were doing, but it soon became apparent that any car, particularly if there was an unaccompanied driver, would happily act as taxi, presumably on payment, giving lifts to and from the centre. There were taxis, to be sure, but not many, and none of them had what could be described as a distinctive livery, other than the presentation of a rickety 'taxi' sign clipped to the roof over the driver's door. Simply standing partially in the road and waving down a car seemed to be entirely acceptable, if slightly dangerous, given that, from my limited experience of Romanian traffic, I had detected a limited degree of road skills.

The closer I got to the city centre, the busier the traffic, although it never became dense. But I could taste, in my mouth, the pollution in the air. There was a gritty, salty, taste to the atmosphere, and I could feel grit in my eyes. There was an overwhelming sense of dirt, whether covering the ground, on the buildings, or hanging in the air. I reflected that one part of the supplies that I was bringing was Pholcodine linctus, and that Mary Gibson had spoken of the children suffering constant upper respiratory tract infections. Now I thought I knew why.

I walked on, deeper into the city, until, on my left, I came to an otherwise unremarkable narrow road, Strada Jules Michelet, one of many names which I was to come across with a French derivation, and which I knew was the address of the British embassy. I turned into the road and, after less than a hundred yards, saw the entrance on the right-hand side. Standing at the pedestrian gate next to a comparatively run-down sentry box was an overweight perspiring policeman, fending off the attentions of a dozen or so supplicants who were attempting to gain access. I walked straight up to him, and flashed my British passport, and he jerked his head towards the building, allowing me past.

No sooner had I passed through the gates than the scene changed abruptly from one of noise, dust and grime to the cool of landscaped gardens which could have been transported straight from Kensington Palace. Manicured lawns, well-ordered and beautifully maintained flower beds and even, I imagined, a strutting peacock greeted my eye. I thought I heard rather than saw the trickle of water from a fountain.

I walked round the side of the building, following the signs to the consulate, and found myself in what appeared to be a wooden side extension. The mirage of calm and tranquillity was immediately shattered. I was in a long, narrow, room, with, at the end, a counter, shielded from the public by glass partitions. There appeared to be two clerks at the counter, while on my side, men and women seethed in some sort of disorganised scrum, attempting to push their way to the counter through people already present and equally determined to stand their ground.

It was starting to become clear that there was no such thing in Romania as a queue. It seemed that the noisier and more physically aggressive one could be, the more likely it would be that the destination would be reached earlier.

It was pretty obvious that everyone in the room was there for one purpose – to obtain a visa or some sort of entry permit into the United Kingdom. On each wall were notices in English and Romanian making it perfectly plain that a visa would not be granted unless the applicant was sponsored – that is, that they could identify a United Kingdom resident who was prepared to confirm that money would be available to the applicant to ensure his or her support while in the United Kingdom and a speedy return at the end of the stay, without recourse to welfare benefits.

Given that any idea of queuing was out of the question, it dawned on me that it was pointless waiting at the back of the room, and so, by a series of deft manoeuvres, adopting the Romanian system of pushing, shoving and squeezing, and given that I was on my own rather than, as it seemed, one of a couple or trio or even more members of a family, I managed to worm my way to the counter after some 15 minutes of endeavour.

As I stood in front of the glass, I was still buffeted from side to side by the human throng behind me, but I stood my ground and tried to make myself heard through the partition. I put my passport on the counter.

"I am English and have just arrived in Bucharest. I am seeking to adopt a child from an orphanage and I gather that I should report into the embassy to make sure that I am following the correct procedure."

The clerk looked at me blankly. In heavily accented English, she said, "We close at 5pm."

I looked at the clock. It showed 4:45pm. I was a little unclear as to how that was supposed to answer my question. So I changed tack. I remembered the name which Ian Marriott had given me.

"I am told that I should ask to see Kirsty Rowe, the vice consul. May I please have a word with her?"

The clerk turned to her companion and said something which I could not catch, given the cacophony behind me, and a moment later she pointed to one side of the room, close to the counter, and told me to wait.

Ten minutes later, a side door opened, and a woman gestured me inside and into an office which turned out to be that of the vice consul.

"What can I do for you?" she said.

I explained that I was following what I took to be the appropriate procedure, given that I and my mother had come to Bucharest in the hope of adopting a child. I understood that I had to present myself to the embassy at the outset.

Without a hint of either approval or disapproval, she said, "It is complicated. The law here is unclear and may well change. Her Majesty's government is doing its best to keep up with developments in this country, but at the same time, there are very strict procedures which you have to follow."

"I'm aware of that, and I know that the embassy has to liaise with both the Home Office and the Department of Health in London before I can hope to have a child enter the UK. But I think I have been following the requirements so far and indeed I have already had a home study report undertaken which has been positive and that has been forwarded to the Department of Health in London by my local authority."

For some reason, Miss Rowe did not seem to take particularly kindly to this information or the steps which I had already taken. However, I ignored her marked lack of enthusiasm, and ploughed on. "My next step, as I understand it, is to identify a child or children, and that is what I propose to do. When I have done that, I will come back and arrange an appointment so that the necessary formalities can be pursued."

She looked at me coolly. "You'll not be able to take any child out of the country and into the United Kingdom without entry clearance."

I knew that, having read the guidance issued by the Department of Health from cover to cover. Indeed, a letter to that effect was part of my dossier, but I was slightly taken aback by the tone of her voice. There was the faintest suggestion that to get entry clearance would be highly unlikely, or, at best, would be something of a struggle.

I had hoped that she would at least appear to be taking some sort of written note of our conversation and that she might give a word either of encouragement or of advice, but she did not give any hint at all of support, and seemed to express no interest at all in what I was about. She brought an end to our conversation immediately.

She rose from her seat behind the desk. "You can arrange an appointment through the office or by telephone," she said and gave me a card with the embassy number on it.

So that was that. I had registered my interest and my presence. I didn't know quite what I expected, and I sensed a certain antipathy in the embassy response, but putting it down to my imagination, I left the fragrant gardens behind, and emerged once more into the dusty city streets of Bucharest. Perhaps, over optimistically, I had thought that the embassy would be not simply sympathetic to but somehow naturally supportive of efforts to rescue the children from the orphanages, but I had a horribly empty feeling that perhaps the embassy was not, as it were, on our side at all.

It was just after 5pm, and, true to its word, the consular office had shut and the clamour had ended when I left the vice consul's office. It was time to return to the hotel, make sure that my mother was alright, and then move on to my next step, which was to find the translator, Lily.

***

I retraced my steps out of the city, remarking to myself that there didn't seem to be such a thing as a 'rush hour', since the volume of traffic had, if anything, reduced. It was still stiflingly hot, and by the time I returned to the hotel, my T-shirt was wet through with perspiration. The good news, however, was that my mother was rested and we both decided that we would establish whether or not there was any likelihood of a meal being available, and we returned to reception. Mircea directed us to the hotel dining room without great enthusiasm, and I soon discovered why. It was totally incongruous, bearing in mind the size of the hotel and its design, and comprised nothing more than a small room made out in some curious faux Baroque style, with only about twenty tables. Apart from the two of us, the room was completely empty.

We sat down and waited. Eventually, a waitress appeared who was unable to communicate with us in either French or English and who was utterly bewildered by the suggestion that there might be a menu. The only food available, it appeared, was that which we had experienced on the flight – some cold ham and perhaps some tomatoes. We could have water to drink. And sure enough, some pretty unappetising boiled ham was placed before us with a small dish of tomatoes and a jug of water. My mother ate virtually nothing. For my part, perhaps fortunately, I like tomatoes, and I was reasonably content with the ham once I had removed its generous coating of fat;   my exertions that afternoon had given me a substantial appetite, so I set to, ignoring the modest nature of our meal.

Our eating habits, let alone our appetites, were going to have to change pretty rapidly.

We didn't stay long in our dining room and, in any event, we both knew that we had to move on the next day to Bacau, so my mother decided on an early night. I asked the receptionist about directions to the domestic airport which I knew we had to find for the next leg of our trip.

"You want to go to Baneasa Airport," he said. "It's closer than Otopenei – and in fact you will probably hear aeroplanes landing and engines warming up from your room. But you'll need a taxi to get there, and I must warn you, if there is anything that works to time in Romania, it is the domestic airport, which makes sure that all planes leave and arrive exactly in accordance with the timetable."

"Can you arrange a taxi for us to get there?"

He pursed his lips. "Of course, I can try. But remember what I said. The plane will leave on time."

***

Meanwhile, I had more work to do. An immediate task was to find Lily, the translator who, Ian had assured me, could translate my home study report in short order. I had telephoned her from England, and she had assured me that she would be at home and I could drop my documents round to her on the evening of my arrival. So, leaving my mother to get some rest, I set off once more, and mimicking the custom which I had seen earlier in the day, I managed to flag down a car masquerading as a taxi which took me to the housing estate where the interpreter's flat could be found.

Carrying an anonymous-looking carrier bag with my home study report and my dossier inside it, I found my way to the third floor of what seemed to be the right block and rang the bell. Sure enough, Lily was waiting for me, although in the most extraordinary state of undress. I had to make allowances for the oppressive temperature of this summer's evening, but I was still surprised to see that she was wearing little more than a blouse and some sort of panties, and seemed quite unconcerned that everything else was bare.

Nonetheless, her language skills were evident, and she invited me into her flat and had me sit in her living room while she looked over my paperwork.

"I can translate all this," she said, "and it will be ready for you by the end of the week." I should collect them, she said, from the office where she worked, in central Bucharest, in the office of 'the Notary'.

I handed over the agreed fee, in dollars, which she stuffed into a purse.

That seemed to be that. How, then, was I to find my way back to the hotel, given that I was now out in the suburbs?

"You can get a bus or a tram," she said. "If you walk out of the estate and towards the main road you will see a bus line which you can catch into the town centre."

I pointed out that it was by now night-time, and I had completely lost my sense of direction.

"Oh, there's no problem," she said. "You will see a bus or a tram from the end of the road leading here, and that will take you back to the centre."

Was there a route number? Lily gave me a number but of course the same number would also be travelling in the opposite direction. She insisted, however, that it would be obvious when the right bus came along. I was not particularly keen on climbing onto a Romanian bus without the faintest idea of either the route I should be following or the destination I should choose, but I decided to hide my trepidation, thanked Lily, and made my way downstairs.

In fact, by now it was not only completely dark, but there was virtually no street lighting of any sort. I would learn, much later, that such was the cost of fuel for the country's power stations, every effort was made to conserve energy, and street lighting was considered not to be essential. Such illumination as there was came from the windows of the flats and houses around me, and when I found my way onto the surrounding streets, I soon found that I was walking in pitch blackness. With no street lighting that I could make out, there was no reflecting glow from the sky, and without any moonlight to speak of, I was close to blind.

Nonetheless, I struck out as confidently as possible, knowing, from what I'd seen as we had driven to the estate earlier, that there were virtually no other pedestrians around and so it was highly unlikely that I would actually bump into anyone. At one stage, I came across a large roundabout which boasted a dim street light and saw a couple of bus passengers waiting in a shelter. I went across and spoke to them, using just the one word which I imagined would pass muster

"Centru?" I said, pointing in the direction which I was following.

They both nodded, smiling, giving me, at least, the confidence to carry on. And so I walked on, in darkness which was punctuated from time to time by the dim light of a house window and, less frequently, by vestiges of moonlight which revealed itself through brief breaks in the clouds overhead.

Then, suddenly, I felt compelled to stop. I had no idea why, but something urged me not to take one step further. I could vaguely make out on my right-hand side that there was a high wall which I must have been following for a good number of yards. To my left, I knew, was the street.

I have often read of the hairs on the back of the neck transmitting some sort of alert, a sensation which I confess I have never experienced, mainly because my neck is devoid of hair. But certainly, I had encountered something which compelled me to stop, and as I struggled to get my bearings and work out quite what had alerted me, down the road from behind me came an ancient tram, scattering showers of sparks as it lost and then renewed connection with the overhead wires.

One such shower burst close to where I was standing, illuminating the path ahead. Where there was no path at all. I had stopped right on the edge of the pavement by a sunken entry to what appeared to be a factory gate on my right. The sunken entry was in fact a steep decline down which delivery lorries would no doubt negotiate their passage into the factory itself. The incline appeared to be extremely steep – from initially the same level as the roadway, it seemed to descend to a depth of 6 feet or more across the width of the pavement. Since I was walking along the middle of the pavement, I would have walked, without any warning, into a drop of at least 3 feet and I would very probably have been significantly injured.

No doubt, during daylight hours, there was some sort of warning of this chasm. And it appeared that at night-time, pedestrians obviously chose not to frequent the streets of Bucharest, given the lack of illumination. For my part, I was pretty shaken up but also incredibly fortunate, and while I cannot pretend to have a sixth sense, something had alerted me and protected me from what could have been an early catastrophe. Coincidence? Radar? Goodness knows, but I was a very lucky man.

I decided to skirt around the entrance way and continue my journey walking in the street. When I had completed another mile or so, I came across what appeared to be a rather larger square, with at least some faint lighting, and obviously much closer to the centre. I again copied the actions of those wanting lifts and flagged down a car for a ride into the city.

As I had observed already, most drivers appeared perfectly willing to offer a lift to passers-by, and the one who stopped for me was even more eager when I indicated that I was prepared to give him a dollar to take me to Hotel Parc. Of course, at the black-market rate of exchange, I was giving him the equivalent of several hundred lei – an unheard-of amount for a relatively short trip across town, but it satisfied us both for our separate reasons. He spoke neither English nor French, but with my little hotel map I was able to make my destination clear enough just as he was able to explain by means of sign language, shrugs and a stab at the petrol gauge ten minutes later, that he had run out of petrol. Feeling sorry for him, and buoyed up by my recent experience with the factory gate, I gave him another dollar, assuming that that would help him fill the tank, and I happily waited in his car while he walked off with a petrol can, equipment which I assumed was pretty important in a time of shortages.

Ultimately, and rather later than I had planned, I arrived back at Hotel Parc, close to midnight. The one thing that our bathroom did boast was a shower, and though the water was tepid and the flow only just above a trickle, it was bliss to wash the dirt of the day off me, wash my hair, and emerge relatively refreshed for my night's sleep.

Back in our room, I told my mother about my experiences and I also warned her about the need to be punctual for the flight the next day. She was still looking a bit the worse for wear.

"Our flight leaves at eight o'clock in the morning, and the receptionist insists that it will leave on time. So I have asked for a taxi at seven and we must be up and ready to catch it."

"Of course," said my mother, making something of an obvious effort not to be tetchy. "I'll be up and ready."

Which in fact turned out to be something of an optimistic overstatement. For my part, I could not sleep at all through the night, and so I was wide awake, though tired, at six o'clock, bustling about, getting things ready for departure. I repacked my case and checked the rucksack and by 6.30 I was ready.

Not so my mother, who appeared to be struggling.

"I'm sorry, Ma, but we really must get on. We have a plane to catch."

Eventually, she struggled out of bed, gathered her things together and followed me downstairs to reception. Thankfully, she only had one case and, since she appeared not to be in any state to carry it, I made myself cope with that and, to her obvious relief, I took hold of mine while shouldering my rucksack without too much difficulty. But where was our taxi? It was nowhere to be seen.

I was beginning to realise that if there was any form of regulation of taxis, it was probably ignored, given that I now had experience of most car owners moonlighting their services, particularly to foreigners who would be prepared to pay in dollars.

I went across to the reception desk and asked whether any taxi had been ordered for us. I realised, as I spoke, that I was making an assumption that there was such a thing as a radio taxi network, which, on reflection, was absurd, but I still harboured a hope that somehow, although I knew not how, a taxi might have been found to take us across to the airport.

I half expected the answer. There was no taxi, but perhaps one could be found within a few minutes. Another receptionist, who had not been on duty the night before, came out onto the front steps and looked vaguely towards the main road. It seemed that that was the best that he, and indeed we, could do. The quest was hopeless. Finally, I realised that there was nothing for it: we should look for a car with a single driver, flag him down, and simply ask whether or not he would be prepared to act as a taxi for us.

And that, eventually, is how we managed to get a ride to the airport. And perhaps it also explains how it is that we got there too late to catch our flight, which, as I had been alerted the night before, left at exactly eight o'clock.

TEN

"Fortune soon tires of carrying any one long on her shoulders."

Gracián, *The Art of Worldly Wisdom*, 1647

The official at the check-in desk was sympathetic and, mercifully, spoke French. I asked him whether there was another departure for Bacau that day.

"Bien sur."

When?

"A deux heures."

Was there room on the flight?

"Certainement."

And, without any fuss, he assured us that we could both join the flight provided we returned no later than one o'clock. A scruffy-looking man in a faded blue jacket with several days' stubble on his chin offered to take our cases. Where were we going, and when? I told him, causing him great hilarity when I mispronounced Bacau. He thought it highly amusing that I should think of travelling to Baku, which I later realised was in Russia. However, he made it plain that we could leave our cases on shelving in the departure hall. No doubt I looked as doubtful as I felt, whereupon he smiled broadly, revealing one tooth. He insisted, in broken and guttural French, that there would be no problem and he would personally keep an eye on our possessions.

Leaving them with some trepidation, we emerged from the airport and found a motorist who was eager to take us into the city for a dollar, and I suggested that we might have a look round in the time available to us. It was plain, however, by the time we got past the outskirts, that my mother was not really in a fit state to go sightseeing. She was short of breath and found it difficult to walk at any pace, let alone any distance and so we found our way to what appeared to be some sort of hotel coffee bar which served just that – cups of weak instant coffee supplemented, if we chose, by a limited number of soft drinks. There did not appear to be anything to eat.

A waiter served our drinks and, realising that we were foreigners, immediately attempted to sell lei to us. To keep things sweet, I handed over five dollars for a similar size of wad that I had received on the minibus.

"Ma," I said, "I suggest I go for a walk round to see what's up, while you take a rest here." She nodded weakly, pleased enough simply to remain resting at the table while I walked out into what appeared to be one of the main thoroughfares of Bucharest.

The immediate and overwhelming impression was one of grime and deprivation. Everything, from the buildings to the traffic, and in particular the occasional heavy-goods lorry, varied only in degrees of dirt. The hardship, if not already apparent, was accentuated by the immediate attention of a series of children with their hands out, begging for money. Initially, I felt compelled to give them something, but this simply magnified their attention and, after handing out what coins I had, it was necessary to escape their approaches by following the example of other pedestrians, who simply ignored them.

There were shop fronts of various sizes along the sides of the street I first came to, but the windows, where they were not boarded up, revealed nothing. Either the interiors of all the buildings were shrouded in darkness or there was, from time to time, an uninviting display of such unpleasant-looking goods as to put off any prospective customer from going inside. I saw a tailor's dummy, dressed in a suit of clothes which I imagined would have been *de rigeur* on a Communist party platform in the 1950s. But I saw no electrical store, no café or restaurant, no convenience store, nor even a grocery store or the like, save, that is, for one, which I came across on one of the street corners. A shop with a wide, open doorway but which initially appeared to be in darkness, revealed itself as open for business. On closer inspection, I could just ascertain, in the gloom, on a wooden table, a few upended crates of tomatoes.

I slipped down some side streets to see if there was such a thing as a baker's shop or a dairy. There was none.

In one square, set back from the main road, I came across what appeared to be the Opera House. What had once been a handsome and ornate building was now boarded up and looked in a very sorry state. The gardens to the front and side were overgrown and bedraggled. A notice board to the front of the building was bare except for one faded and torn poster from which it was quite impossible to make out what was being advertised or when.

Back on another main street, I looked up at the first-floor windows and saw pockmarks and bullet holes on building after building, continuing evidence of the aftermath of scattered but substantial small-arms fire. Clearly, in the panic of revolution, adrenaline-fuelled soldiers or rebels had simply pointed their weapons at windows, loosing off hails of gunfire, assuming, probably rightly, that if only a percentage of ordnance found its way through the openings, that would be enough to either kill or maim. There was no evidence of any attempt at refurbishment.

From time to time, I came across a street hawker, selling everything from cigarettes to soap, surrounded by a dozen or so passers-by, themselves keen to get hold of provisions which were obviously not on sale in any form of retail outlet.

It seemed, in this briefest of snapshots, that I had been transported back to my infancy, to a Europe trying to come to terms with the immediate aftermath of global conflict. Perhaps this was what citizens had to endure in their former life in East Berlin – or indeed any post-war Communist regime. The scene was utterly depressing, and a bewildering and stark contrast to the life to which I had become accustomed in England

I walked slowly back through the streets to the hotel bar and sat down opposite my mother, who did her best to be cheerful.

"I'm not hungry," she protested an answer to my concern. "Let's get back to the airport and make sure that we don't miss this flight!"

And so, for another dollar, we returned to the airport and I found a vending trolley which enabled me to buy her a drink and a curious-looking biscuit. We had been away for some four hours, and our possessions were intact and so I sat by them, gloomily considering our next step.

***

According to my plan, I had now to find my way to Doctor Sadovici and, hopefully, the English nurse whose name and address I had on my itinerary. I had the name of the hotel into which we had been booked, and it was now just a question of waiting for the flight.

As the hour or so to our departure passed, my spirits lightened. I find travel almost as exciting as my mother, and I am always engaged by the sight of departure boards which speak of exotic-sounding destinations and which, by their names alone, carry a sense of mystery. I once spent an entire evening in the *Train Blue* restaurant in the Gare de Lyon in Paris dreamily looking down at the departure boards at the *tete de station*, while my bouillabaisse turned cold, watching passengers embarking for Madrid, Berne, Rome, Nice, Marseilles and other gloriously mysterious cities whose names so excited my imagination. For now, of course, I was in a domestic airport, handling only internal flights, but I immediately recognised one of the destinations – Timisuara – the town which, from news reports, had proved itself to be one of the powder kegs of the revolution.

Eventually, and, of course, bang on time, our flight was called. Each passenger handed over the boarding cards which had been given out at the check-in desk. Every single one of them had been used many times before and were dog-eared and, seemingly, from a host of different airlines. Mine, for reasons which I simply could not guess at, bore the PanAm logo.

We found our way on to a monoplane with an enormous engine and propeller at the front. The aircraft must have been decades old, but as I realised more and more during my odyssey, one particular skill which Romanians had had to learn was to mend and adapt, conserving, repairing, and making the best of that which was available. The plane may well have been very old, but it was serviceable, if rather uncomfortable, and, whatever its age, it was clearly being maintained very carefully. We clambered up the steps under the fixed overhead wing and found our way to our seats and buckled ourselves in. We were followed by an air hostess whose presence remained a mystery throughout the flight, since there was no form of in-flight catering, and what appeared to be three pilots. Two climbed into the pilot and co-pilot seats and the third leaned on his stomach, almost spread-eagled between the two of them, on the raised cowling which appeared to accommodate what I assumed were the aircraft controls, the cables, connections, and links to that enormous engine.

***

For all the antiquity of the aeroplane, the flight was both uneventful and comparatively smooth. The pilots left their communicating door wide open, presumably to improve the air quality in their cramped cabin, while the engine set up such a racket that it was impossible to hear oneself think. However, for all its apparent antiquity and design, the crew treated the machine almost lovingly and the pilot completed the softest of landings on the grass strip which served Bacau and taxied across to the 'terminal', a small wooden building which appeared to pass muster as an office and waiting room. There were only some dozen or so passengers on the flight, and I guessed that we were all expected to cram ourselves into a waiting minibus. I showed the driver my hotel reservation coupon and he nodded, gesturing us both inside.

The minibus jolted into life and off we set, out of the grassed area, onto the paved roads of Bacau, and into the town centre. The town appeared to be of a comparatively modest size, with one main thoroughfare of some length. When the time came for us to disembark, we found ourselves at one end, opposite our destination hotel, the Moldova, whose name was partially obscured by a large Russian tourist bus.

I knew that we were close to the border with Moldavia and, by definition, what was left of the Iron Curtain. That didn't alarm me – if anything, it added a sense of mystery to my expedition.

The heat of the afternoon was almost overpowering, certainly for my mother, but I managed to get her and our luggage across the street into the entrance of the hotel, where I deposited her. I stood up and looked around me. Stretching back from the entrance was what appeared to be a wide, low hall of some length, in semi-darkness but with some illumination at the far end. That, as far as I could make out, was the reception area to which I made my way. There, I found a receptionist engaged in lively conversation with, given my limited knowledge of the accent and phraseology, a man who I assumed to be a Russian tourist.

I stood, patiently, while the two of them talked for some time, until finally the receptionist looked across at me without the faintest sense of welcome.

"Do you speak English?"

"Nu."

"Parlez-vous Français?"

"Oui."

Well, that was something.

"J'ai une réservation—"

He interrupted. "Non. Vous n'avez pas une réservation."

I was struck by his immediate hostility which I simply could not fathom. He had no idea, I assumed, who I was, and he had not even seen my reservation coupon which I now dug out of my pocket and pushed towards him.

He ignored it. "Encore," he said. "Vous n'avez pas une réservation."

In the face of this unpleasantness, I struggled to produce the most erudite response from my crumbling French vocabulary. "Regardez mon billet," I stumbled.

"Ça n'est pas une réservation," he replied, before making a great show of returning to the conversation with the Russian. Clearly, any dialogue with me was now at an end.

I was completely nonplussed and for a moment had no idea what to do, and turned back towards the hotel entrance. As I did so, a figure detached itself from the wall in one of the darker corners of the hallway and came across to me. It turned out to be a young man whom I had not seen when I first entered the reception area but who was now taking something of an interest in my predicament.

"On vous aide, Monsieur?" he said, as he sidled up to me. Given that I was completely confused by what had just happened, my defences were down and I replied that yes, he might be able to help.

I explained that I and my mother had arrived from England and that we had a reservation at this hotel and the receptionist had made it plain, somehow, that we did not and that at that moment I was at something of a loss as to the next step.

His French was probably no better than mine, but we were able to make ourselves understood reasonably well and he made it plain that he knew of another hotel in Bacau where he was certain we could find accommodation. For my part, I had absolutely no idea what he was talking about but, given that I had no other option, I allowed him to lead on and show me where it was thought that my mother and I would find rooms.

I paused at the entrance and told my mother in very brief terms that there appeared to have been some sort of mix-up but that I and this young man would be seeking a way to resolve it. For her part, she was obviously so fed up that she did not think to ask how it was that this complete stranger could somehow sort out our problem. Leaving her with our luggage at the entrance of the Hotel Moldova, I struck out after the young man, who led me back up the main street almost to the very end, where he pointed to a rather more modern-looking building, announcing itself as Hotel President. He beckoned me inside and we found our way to the main reception desk. An elegant-looking woman behind the desk had the grace to smile at me, which was a good start. When I introduced myself as a traveller from England and explained that there appeared to have been some mix-up with our hotel reservation she asked my name.

"But of course," she exclaimed in French, "we have your reservation here."

She looked over my reservation coupon with obvious approval while I stood perplexed but relieved, wondering what more oddities were to surface. I explained that I would have to go and get my mother and my luggage, while the receptionist, eager to please and continue the welcome, told me that there was no hurry and she would be pleased to see me as soon as I returned.

So, I and this curious but as yet anonymous young man turned on our heels and returned to the street.

I felt I had to at least show some gratitude for his help, and I offered him one of the packs of Kent, which he eagerly accepted. What, he asked, was I doing in Romania? Was it a holiday or business?

Taken somewhat off my guard, I told him exactly why I and my mother were in Romania and, as my story unfolded, he became more and more interested in my endeavour.

"I can find you a child," he said, as I finished. "In fact, I am sure that I can find you two."

I was immediately on my guard. How did he think he could find a child? Indeed, who was he? That he should have been hanging round the other hotel, and should have then led me to this one, to which my reservation had been moved, seemed like a coincidence too far.

"Don't worry," he said, seeing my immediate hesitation. "I know of mothers who cannot afford to keep their children and who wish to have them adopted by good people like you."

I confess that I didn't care for this at all, and that my unease was growing. I explained that I already had a plan, which involved seeing someone in Bacau and possibly visiting an orphanage.

He seemed disappointed that I did not jump at his suggestion, but he said that if I did need further help I should contact him, and he gave me a card with his telephone number. Then he simply melted away.

I put him out of my mind and, back at Hotel Moldova, I told my mother that our hotel had changed, but we did have rooms after all, and that if she could walk with me back up the street, we would find somewhere to rest very shortly.

Without much enthusiasm, she got to her feet and, as we were about to leave, a harassed-looking man whom I took to be the hotel manager approached. Thankfully, he spoke English. "Can I help you? Is there a problem?" he asked.

I told them that I had had a reservation at his hotel, just as the coupon, which I showed him, confirmed, but that his receptionist had dismissed me out of hand. I explained that I felt that the treatment had been, at the very least, impolite.

The manager was profuse in his apologies. "That is unforgivable," he said. "Come with me and I am sure that we can sort it out for you."

I was almost in two minds, but I decided that, having received at least what appeared to be a cordial welcome from Hotel President, and since, for reasons which I simply could not comprehend, they appeared to have my reservation, I should stay, now, in that hotel, so I thanked the manager for his concern and told him not to worry further.

He was disappointed, he said, and backed away, clearly upset that I had been treated poorly, but I detected a sense of relief that I was not going to create a scene. Instead, I hoisted my rucksack on my shoulders again, took our other two cases, and led my mother back up the main street.

ELEVEN

"The child, for the full and harmonious development of his or her personality, should grow up in a family environment, in an atmosphere of happiness, love and understanding."

United Nations Convention on the Rights of the Child, *Resolution 44/25* of 20 November 1989

The walk back up the main street in Bacau took us some time, with several stops. The heat, and my mother's lack of stamina, turned this second trip to the other end of town into something of a route-march, but we finally arrived, tired and dishevelled, at the reception desk which I had left earlier that afternoon. The friendly receptionist was still there and welcomed us back. She was sure that we'd want something to eat and she would arrange that for us. What would we like, steak and chips?

I began to salivate just at the thought. At last, things appeared to be looking up and the picture brightened even more when she asked the purpose of our visit.

"I have travelled here," I said, relaxing into increasingly confident French, "because in England we have heard of the conditions in orphanages in Romania and we are hoping to offer two children a home."

"But that is lovely," she said. "And how do you propose to start?"

I told her that I been given the name of Dr Sadovici.

She interrupted me. "Dr Sadovici? But I know his wife. I speak to her every day. I will contact her immediately and arrange for you see her husband."

Things were definitely improving. I told her that we would go to our room, unpack and come back down to tea and she could perhaps then tell us of the outcome of her call to Mrs Sadovici.

I was dying for a shower and quite obviously my mother needed to cool off too, so we made our way to our room and unpacked.

The room was very much like the room in Hotel Parc, a sort of battered 1960s style, all dark wood and angles, and not in the best of repair, despite its outwardly modern appearance. There was a bathroom, but on turning the tap on, all that came out was a couple of brownish drips and nothing else. So too with the bath. A shower was quite obviously out of the question.

My mother lay down on the bed, exhausted. For my part, I was more excited than tired, bearing in mind that suddenly we had a breakthrough.

"Come on," I said. "Let's get something to eat."

At least the thought of food generated some enthusiasm in my mother and we found our way to the tiny dining room, just off the reception area, where the receptionist herself waited on our table.

Sure enough, she produced steak and chips which we set upon immediately. The steak was probably horse but was succulent enough, and after two days of eating virtually nothing, I was absolutely ravenous. That, with ice cream to follow was, at that moment, a meal fit for a king.

The next step, of course, was to make contact with the English nurse who had been identified to me as Meg Bennett by the Romanian Orphanage Trust. She had a room in a Hotel Dumbrava, somewhere in the area, and I showed the address to our friendly receptionist. She knew exactly where it was and gave me directions to get there, on foot, from the hotel.

"And," she said, "I have good news. Dr Sadovici will come here at nine o'clock tomorrow morning and will meet you at the hotel."

I thanked her profusely and, while my mother made her way slowly upstairs, I walked out of the hotel to find my next contact.

***

The directions were not that difficult to follow since, as I had thought, Bacau was not that large a town. Although the address I had been given was that of a hotel, it was more of a block with small self-contained apartments. Meg Bennett's was on the first floor. And when I got to her door, it was open, and I could hear a young man's voice, speaking in broken English, offering to give help to transport children to activities which he would be pleased to supervise once he had come back, with his girlfriend, from a trip to the seaside.

I wondered to myself why he should have been planning a trip to the coast when it seemed rather a long way for what appeared to be a day trip, given that we were some considerable distance from the Black Sea coast. Perhaps his outing seemed even odder because of what I was then to be told by Meg. She saw me standing in the doorway when I knocked and put her finger to her lips and gestured for me to sit down and, effectively, to remain silent.

Mystified, I sat through the remainder of her conversation with the young Romanian and when, finally, she was satisfied that he had left and was out of earshot, she turned back to me.

"You're English, aren't you," she stated, almost as a fact.

Surprised, I said that I was.

"It is obvious from your clothes and your hair, and the colour of your skin that you are at least not Romanian. What are you doing here?"

I told her that I had written a lengthy letter, care of her address, to Dr Sadovici, and that I and my mother had come to Bacau in the hope that, with his contacts and his support, we could adopt two Romanian children.

"Frankly," she said, "I wouldn't even try. The Romanians don't care for these adoptions and they don't like the idea that children will be removed from their country."

"Come off it," I said. "You must know more than anybody how deprived and damaged these children are becoming as a result of the failure of the Romanian state to provide them with adequate care."

"Maybe. But removing them from the country takes them away from their birthright."

I had heard quite enough about birthright, and my impatience got the better of me.

"What is this about depriving the Romanian children of anything? Haven't they suffered enough deprivation already? Birthright comes a long way behind the need of the child for the love and care of a family. A child has the right to be cared for and nurtured by a parent. This 'birthright' thing is, in these circumstances, absolutely meaningless. A child who has suffered emotional, social, and intellectual deprivation of the kind that these children are facing wouldn't understand the first thing about the word." I found myself transported back to my meetings with Graham Prestridge in England and again I felt the same sense of frustration.

"I'm sorry," I said. "I'm allowing my feelings to get the better of me."

"Look," she replied. "I'm just warning you about the attitude that the Romanians have. You will find that they don't like you and don't like what you are about. Don't expect them to welcome you with open arms, and be ready for an unpleasant reception."

When I told her that I had written a letter by way of an advance introduction, she told me that, in fact, she had not received any correspondence for forwarding to Dr Sadovici, and it was obvious, therefore, that on meeting him the next day he would be wholly unaware of my background or my motives. That, perhaps, given what she had just told me, might not be such a bad thing.

"We're meeting tomorrow morning," I told her. "I have copies of my proposals and my home study report and I'll show them to him. Maybe I can persuade him that my motives are the best and that any child I bring out of Romania will remain Romanian and will be able to return as and when they want."

"Okay," she said, resignedly. "Just don't say that you haven't been warned."

"And by the way," she continued, as I got up to leave, "you'll need these." She dug into one of a collection of boxes which seemed to take up a good portion of her room and brought out some tablets. "These are water purification pills. Under no circumstances must you touch the water until it has been purified by one pill for every glass. The pollution here is dreadful. The water is drawn from a river which has been destroyed by at least one factory upstream, and it is thoroughly poisonous. And, as you have probably been told, not only is the water polluted, but it is only turned on twice a day, for an hour in the morning and an hour in the early evening."

In fact, I didn't know anything of the sort. Water restrictions were news to me, and there had been no suggestion of that at the hotel, but it explained why nothing came out of the taps. Anyway, grateful for that information and pondering the rather more sobering description of the reception that I was likely to receive, I wished her goodbye and retraced my steps to our hotel.

I walked slowly, in a state of some confusion. I had now been warned twice about antipathy toward adoption in Romania, and now by someone with hands-on experience of life in a Romanian orphanage. What was it that could possibly justify this insistence that the children should not be taken out and cared for in a loving home? I could understand it if there were queues of Romanian families offering care and nurture to these children, but there was not a hint of any help at all from that quarter.

The only person who had appeared at all positive about my plans was the friendly receptionist at our hotel and she at least appeared to be a close friend of the wife of the Director of three such orphanages. I took some comfort from that and tried to dismiss the warnings which I had now received.

Back at the hotel, I desperately wanted a shower or bath and I found that my mother had had exactly the same thought. Whether by luck or design, she had discovered that the taps were running again, and she had endeavoured to fill the bath. Unfortunately, she had succeeded in half filling it with a revolting-looking liquid which appeared to be a brownish effluent that could hardly be dignified by the term 'water'. There was an oily scum on the surface, and a faint smell of petrol filled the bathroom.

"Sorry, Ma, but there's no way either of us is going to get into that. I have just been warned of severe water pollution in this area, as if that warning were needed in the light of what we can see in the bath."

It was so unpleasant that I could not even stand the thought of scrubbing myself down with a flannel, and I elected, simply, to get out of my grubby T-shirt and lie down on the bed thinking about the meeting I had just had and the meeting to come. I decided that it was probably better not to tell my mother of the warning I had received. It was better, I imagined, that she should share my initial optimism about the next day's encounter with Sadovici. So we both settled down to get as much sleep as possible in the clammy heat of the summer's night.

Next morning, I got up and went downstairs and begged two glasses of water from reception so that we could at least clean our teeth. I had told my mother of the need to use the purification tablets, and I told her not to drink anything which had not been purified.

She shot me a stricken look. "I think I may have taken some water without having it purified," she said.

"Well let's hope nothing happens, and let's get some breakfast, if there is any." And down we went to the dining room.

There was breakfast of a sort, comprising black tea and stale rolls of bread with jam, which I simply could not face. I took a sip of tea, hoping that the water had been boiled sufficiently to take away the pollutants, and then suggested that my mother and I should wait in the foyer for Dr Sadovici, since it was approaching nine o'clock.

Our friendly receptionist appeared not to be on duty, but given that my Englishness stood out, it seemed, like a sore thumb, I decided that a formal introduction was probably unnecessary.

My assumption proved right. Shortly after nine o'clock, a smartly dressed middle-aged man, every inch the clinician, appeared next to us. The contrast between us could not be greater. Dressed in a suit, and carrying a small attaché case, Dr Sadovici sat down next to me, already scruffy in jeans and a T-shirt, not quite the professional that I had wanted to present. My hair was a mess, I was unwashed, and I had not had a shave. However, there was no point in presenting excuses and instead I introduced my mother and decided that I should immediately indicate the purpose of my visit.

Sadovici spoke perfect English, and I was able to explain to him that I had written from England, hoping that he would at least have some idea both of my identity and my mission. I realised, of course, that he had never received my letter, but I was able to pass him a copy which thankfully I had brought with me.

"I prepared a letter of introduction in England, and sent it to you, addressed to Meg Bennett, whom I think you know. Unfortunately, it seems that it hasn't arrived. But this is a copy, and I hope it will convince you of my good intentions."

He took the paper from the and read it carefully. After some minutes he asked me what I thought he could do.

"I gather," I said "that you have adopted two children yourself." He nodded. "So you know how important it is to take the children from these orphanages and give them a loving home."

I was not choosing my words well. Of course he knew how important it was, and again, he rather than I had first-hand experience of the conditions these children were enduring. However, he ignored my presumption.

"What you are suggesting is not popular," he said. "You know, Ceauşescu sold children to the French." I didn't, in fact, know that, but then anything was possible under that man's dictatorship. "And some children," he went on, "were taken by traffickers. None of us in Romania wish to see our children removed, to be denied their heritage."

And there it was again, the birthright thing. I tried to reassure him. "I hope you can see from that document that my motives are entirely pure. I have made sure that I have been properly vetted by our own social services. And I can assure you that any child to whom I give a home in England will know where he comes from and will know that he will be supported in returning here at any moment that he chooses.

If Romanian families would come forward and care for the children themselves, if the country could care for the children, I would not be here. Do you honestly feel that care can be found for these children within your country, here and now?"

Sadovici pursed his lips and appeared deep in thought. Eventually, he turned to me.

"Very well, I believe you. I am sure that I can find two children for you. Just wait here and I will return this afternoon, and I will have the children with me."

Much later, in my darker moments, I was to wonder, on reflection, just how that was supposed to work. Was he literally going to hand over two babies in the hotel to me and my mother? Was there to be no formality, no paperwork, no official oversight of any sort? Was it really as simple as that? But at that moment, given his assurance and his apparent sincerity, I asked no questions. I was overjoyed at having convinced him of my good faith and I said, certainly, I would stay where I was, without moving, and I looked forward to seeing him that afternoon.

With the utmost courtesy, he wished me and my mother good day, and left the building.

I was never to see him again.

TWELVE

"The sudden disappointment of a hope leaves a scar
which the ultimate fulfilment of that hope never entirely
removes."

Thomas Hardy in F.E. Hardy,
The Early Life of Thomas Hardy, 1928

Like two increasingly sore thumbs, my mother and
I sat in the large ground floor foyer of the hotel, a
developing object of curious glances and eventually
downright stares from an assortment of young people. We
found ourselves on particularly uncomfortable settees,
covered in leatherette, with no backrest to speak of,
making it virtually impossible to relax. Just as the nurse
had observed, whether or not my mother could blend in
with the background, I certainly could not. I had assumed
that it was not appropriate to wear Levis, since I had heard
that they were virtually unobtainable in Romania, and I
was simply wearing khaki fatigues and a similar coloured
T-shirt, and ankle boots.

In any event, either my skin colour or my hair marked
me out, and throughout the morning I found myself
being approached by a variety of young men who, for

some reason, thought I might be able to advise them on any number of things, from the quality of architectural drawings which one eager young man in particular insisted on showing me, to the meaning of democracy, which a clutch of young people decided to have me explain. The aspiring designer appeared to have a portfolio of sketches of public utilities, buildings, even streetlamps on which he wanted my opinion, which I was wholly unqualified to give. The overall impression was of designs which appeared to date from the very early 1960s and seemed to my eyes to be very dated, but all I could do, given that neither of us spoke each other's language, was nod and smile and make what I hoped were encouraging noises. To the questions concerning democracy I gave the only answer I could think of, given that my mind was on other things.

"For democracy," I said, "read 'accountability'." I was not wholly convinced that this was the best of definitions, or that democracy was necessarily working as well as it might back home, but I recalled that Churchill had said something along the lines that thus far, nothing better appeared to have been found.

At least my interrogators seemed relatively satisfied and went off to discuss my response among themselves.

I noticed one particular group of young men or, should I say, type of young man. They appeared to take no interest in me and my mother at all, but from time to time, I was able to detect that in fact they were watching us extremely carefully. This group were noticeable by the cleanliness of their clothes – invariably tracksuit bottoms and a clean polo shirt and noticeably clean trainers. None of them approached me, and I avoided catching their eyes, surmising that they were quite possibly members of the allegedly disbanded Securitate.

I had heard of the Stasi, the notorious East German secret police, and a friend back in the UK had had a brush with them while touring Europe in his gap year. He had thought it rather exciting to take a trip into East Berlin on a tourist pass, but had complained when he was required to surrender hard currency for East German marks, and had rather wished, after a rather lengthy and unpleasant interrogation, that he had kept his mouth shut.

I had also heard of the Securitate, although not in any detail. Ceauşescu had managed, I knew, to have everyone inform on each other – neighbours, employees, even family members had felt obliged to co-operate, such was their fear of the secret police. Now that the revolution had removed the dictator, what, I wondered, had happened to the secret police? Had they been disbanded or had they simply slunk into the shadows?

My suspicions grew when, midway through the morning, a lorry drew up at the back entrance to the foyer. I was able to see what was going on, because the entirety of the back wall was made of glass. The lorry, it appeared, was delivering a supply of beer, a delivery which, by the look of it, was eagerly awaited by a very significant number of men who were now milling around the lorry itself and inside the lobby.

Of course, I had no idea how often these deliveries took place, but there was a sense that beer was in short supply, because no sooner had the lorry pulled up than a good number of men tried to get on board. Arguments broke out, and two or three groups of men began scuffling with each other.

The scene was utterly bizarre, but did not last long, since a number of the tracksuits weighed in and hauled away the protagonists, so quickly and efficiently that had I not been watching carefully, I would not have seen it happen. There was no blood, and the raised voices melted away so quickly that I wondered whether I had been imagining what I had seen. In any event, the lorry driver and a couple of helpers managed to offload the crates of beer, some into the hotel and some around the side of the building, presumably to other outlets, and eventually, the lorry, now empty, drove away and calm returned to the foyer.

I decided that I would keep a surreptitious eye on the tracksuits. And each time I glanced across at them, they appeared to have decided, likewise, that at least one would be able to observe me and my mother.

Fortunately, she had brought reading material with her, and she was able, at least in part, to relax. I, too, had a book, but there was no way I could possibly concentrate, given Sadovici's promise. Was I really going to receive two infants that afternoon? Looking back, the idea was absurd, but then again, so was the whole endeavour. What on earth did I think I was doing, sitting in a foreign hotel in a strange land, waiting for a man, however apparently reputable, to suddenly produce two children for me to remove to a country three thousand miles away? I was racked with conflicting emotions – on the one hand, the absurdity of the situation, but on the other, my memory of the dreadful television programmes I had seen and the task Carmel and I had set ourselves.

So, we waited.

***

The afternoon heat became more and more intense and the lack of air conditioning magnified the oppressive atmosphere. Nor could I detect where I might find a drink, and so I simply sat, in increasing discomfort, waiting for Sadovici's return. I looked around the lobby and the ground floor of the hotel and, for want of anything better to do, I tried to take an interest in the building. That itself was pretty depressing, since whatever effort had been made to keep up the maintenance of the hotel seemed to have been approached in a pretty haphazard fashion. Thus, the lift did not work in this hotel either, and although the facings on the walls of the public areas appeared to be some form of marble, I took particular notice of a pillar where a careless worker, whether electrician or otherwise, had installed a light switch after making a hole in the marble that was too big for the fitment. Consequently, the plate housing the switch had had to be screwed onto the wall at a crazy angle from the vertical, leaving the hole behind it visible on two sides.

That switch appeared to me to be a metaphor for the general run-down appearance of virtually every building that I was to come across during my stay, and it seemed to symbolise the reluctance of anyone to complete a job with any skill and with any sense of satisfaction.

As the afternoon wore on and evening descended, it

became pretty plain that there was to be no development. Sadovici simply did not appear, and I was unable to establish what might have happened to him or his promise, because our friendly receptionist was obviously not on duty. And so I sat through the remainder of the day, increasingly frustrated and more and more uncomfortable, until, finally, darkness fell.

At around seven o'clock, my mother had had enough. She went off to the dining room to see if she could get anything to eat, but I told her that I was not going to give up my vigil and, in any event, I was not hungry. She must have found something, because she was away for a little while, before finally coming back to see me sitting, as before, with my eye fixed on the hotel entrance.

"I'm going to bed," she said. "Frankly, I don't think he's going to be coming back today and you really ought to get something to eat and go to bed yourself."

"You might be right, but for the time being, I'm staying put. I'll be up later. Anyway, in this heat I really don't have any appetite."

'Later' turned into very late, because I finally elected to go back to our room at 10 o'clock, pretty fed up and enormously disappointed. There was not much I could say, so I simply climbed into bed and tried to sleep.

***

Next morning, hardly refreshed, I took my mother downstairs and installed her in the dining room to contemplate another stale roll and black tea. Meanwhile, I went back to the reception desk, having seen that our receptionist was back on duty.

"Bonjour," I said, greeting her as cheerfully as I could.

She looked at me icily. Her whole demeanour had changed, and I felt as unwelcome, this early morning, as I had felt welcome two days before.

I told her that I had expected Dr Sadovici to have returned the previous day, since that was what he had promised.

"Je vous assure qu'il est venu," she said.

I wondered if I had misheard her and that somehow I had mistranslated her French.

"Non," I said. "Il n'est pas revenu."

"Ce n'est pas vrai," she insisted. "Il est revenu hier, l'après midi."

I was getting nowhere, and her whole demeanour was becoming more and more hostile.

"De toute façon," she said, "il vous a laissé un message. Vous devez partir."

I was stunned. Had I heard her right? Was she seriously saying that not only had Sadovici turned up the previous afternoon but that, having failed to find me, had left me a message, effectively telling me to get out of town?

"Comment?" I said, asking her to repeat what she had just told me.

"Vous devez partir. On doit aller. Aujourd'hui," she hissed. The other receptionist looked over at us, enquiringly, before returning to his own business.

Things had become pretty plain. She was telling me to get out, and her message was uncompromising. So also was her body language. It was obviously a waste of time to argue the issue with her and I retreated, wondering what on earth I was to do now.

First of all, of course, I had to tell my mother, whom I found in the dining room contemplating the remains of a pretty unappetising piece of bread.

"I'm afraid that things have got a bit out of hand," I said. "The receptionist alleges that Sadovici came back yesterday, which, of course, you and I know he didn't. And she has told me that he has made it plain that we have to leave. Since Sadovici is apparently someone in authority, and discretion being the better part of valour, I suggest that we take that advice and I go to the airline office and get a ticket for us both so that we can return to Bucharest."

"I agree," said my mother after a moment. She appeared relieved to be leaving Bacau. "I'll get packing and I'll wait for you back in the foyer."

I walked straight out of the hotel and made my way to the Tarom office, which I had passed on my way to see Meg Bennett on our first evening, and managed to communicate to the clerk that I needed two one-way tickets to Bucharest that afternoon. For a moment, I wondered whether the flight might be full. Was there even a flight? I needn't have worried; for the ludicrously modest sum of 300 lei each, I emerged from the building with two small pieces of printed cardboard – rather like old British Railways tickets – and the knowledge that we had only to wait for two hours before the next flight.

I collected my mother and our pieces of luggage and went back to reception. The receptionist waved us away, wholly unconcerned with any check-out procedure, leaving me with an abiding sense that I had somehow acted like some sort of criminal. I felt so uneasy that I imagined that I might have a tap on my shoulder from one of the tracksuits, and I only breathed more easily when a taxi – this time found waiting outside the hotel, and accepting lei as a fare – deposited us back at the airfield.

We both sat out our waiting time in the wooden shed that I had seen on arrival, in the company of a handful of other passengers and under the gaze of a dull-looking young soldier who sported a sub-machine gun. Quite what he was guarding escaped me, and probably eluded him, too; he was clearly as bored as I was frustrated.

And then, out of the blue, a soft "Bonjour".

I looked round, startled. Standing just behind me was the curious young man who had approached me at Hotel Moldova. I wondered what on earth he was doing there. Had he followed me? Had he asked at the hotel where I was? Was he rather more than he seemed to be?

I suppose I was feeling a little paranoid by then, but just as it seemed that I could not trust Sadovici, a professional man with seemingly impeccable credentials, this casually dressed young person, who seemed to me to be just a little shifty, was someone I felt I should be just a little wary of.

He gestured me away from the other passengers and into a corner of the room.

"Je vous ai trouvé un enfant," he said.

I have found you a child.

I must have looked pretty perplexed. I had not sent him on a mission and not even agreed that he should find a child. The idea that I would take a child from a family was not just bizarre, it was abhorrent. I had travelled to Romania to bring two children out of squalor, not away from a caring family.

He continued, in French. "I have spoken to the mother and she says that she is too poor to care for the child and she wants you to take him out of Romania."

This was absurd. I had no wish to meet anybody who simply wished to abandon their child to a complete stranger. I sensed that the conversation would soon turn to money and I felt that it was time to end the discussion there and then. I told him that I was at that moment waiting for the next plane back to Bucharest and that my plans had changed radically. That at least was true, in that I now had no plans of any sort, since all my best endeavours appeared to have come to nothing. I was not, however, prepared to discuss my difficulties with him, and I felt that the least said, the better.

He shrugged his shoulders, as if to say "it's your loss", and turned away. Even when, later, I despaired of getting anywhere, I did not try to seek him out.

Not long afterwards, I heard the sound of an approaching aircraft, well in advance of our advertised departure, and I watched as a gaggle of passengers disembarked and their assorted luggage was loaded onto a trolley. A bowser drove across the field and a mechanic fussed around the engine while another saw to the refuelling. They both completed their tasks in short order, allowing us to leave exactly on time, and in due course, we all, the three pilots and the ubiquitous air hostess, were bumping across the grass field, into the air and on the way back to Bucharest.

THIRTEEN

"A good indignation brings out all one's powers."

Emerson, *Journals*, 1841

Whereas we had planned to stay in Bacau for a week, we were now back in Bucharest without any formal reservation or advance-paid hotel accommodation after only three days. There seemed to be nothing for it but to return to Hotel Parc in the hope that they might have somewhere to put us.

In fact, they did, in our previous room. I confess that I was feeling ever so slightly paranoid, and in my heightened state, I wondered whether that room was itself a room which was dedicated to foreign visitors who could, by some means which I didn't have the strength to investigate, be observed, either by some sort of listening bug or, worse, by some sort of state-run surveillance.

I decided, as soon as we got back to the hotel, that I would have to start over with my search. The Marriotts had told us, back in England, that we should find a taxi, and start visiting orphanages. That, I decided, would simply not work in Bucharest, although I did know that there were several orphanages in the city. However, even though I was not going to adopt that strategy, it was clear that I would have to start somewhere and I decided that I had nothing to lose and probably quite a bit to gain by making contact with the nurses who had been identified by Mary Gibson of the Romanian Orphanage Trust. I remembered that she had told me that the government was putting a number of them up in a hotel close to the centre, and I guessed that if I could find them, they might give me some inkling as to where I might start my search.

Leaving my mother in our room in the hope that some rest would help her, I went down to the reception desk. I found Mircea, ever very eager to engage me in English conversation. He told me that he was planning to travel to England, hoping to find work in a major hotel in the vicinity of 'Kessington' in London. With his ability to speak English, and his ambition to take a hotel management course, he was looking forward to his visit. I felt that it would be unkind to suggest that there was something of a gulf between the apparent expectations of hoteliers in Romania and the demands of management and tourists alike in England, and I did my best to make encouraging noises. My willingness to listen to him appeared to pay dividends, since it appeared to encourage him to devote some time to my often rather dull questions.

Finally I got round to my own questions. "Can you tell me where I can find Hotel Lido?"

"But, of course. Look at this map." He produced a dog-eared tourist map and traced the route for me. "You can, in fact, get there on foot."

That was a relief. I had had my fill of flagging down private cars, although no one seemed to mind, least of all the drivers themselves.

I went back upstairs and decided that I would take my rucksack with perhaps an offering of linctus and Hibiscrub. That, I felt, might at least break the ice.

"I am," I told my mother, "starting from square one. I've been given the names of nurses here, and it would seem to be a waste of time to travel outside Bucharest until I have at least made contact with them. I'm not entirely sure how many orphanages there are in this area, but from what I remember of the list sent to me by the Romanian embassy, there are about five in Bucharest itself. So, wish me luck, and I'll see you later."

"Do take care," she said. I think she had probably been more alarmed by the developments in Bacau than I was.

"Actually," I replied, "when I walked back from the translator the other night, although in pitch darkness, I felt quite safe. There was no hint of muggers or criminal gangs roaming the streets, whether because no one was daft enough to be out in the darkness or not, I know not, but I will, of course, be careful."

Slinging my half-full rucksack over my shoulder, I set out, wondering what was now ahead of me.

***

The walk to the Hotel Lido was, as Mircea had suggested, pretty straight and a good deal shorter than my first walk into the city when I visited the embassy. So I arrived there shortly after what would have been suppertime. It was not the most modern of establishments but seemed comfortable, nonetheless. There was an enormous racket coming from a large downstairs reception room which seemed to be hosting some sort of wedding or other celebration. Guests were enjoying themselves hugely and there appeared to be food and drink in plentiful supply. Above the hubbub, I heard and saw red-faced men and women roaring with laughter and shouting at each other and I saw a waiter push through the merry throng holding a tray high above his head on which I could see ranks of cooked vegetables.

I shook my head in disbelief. Here again was another contrast between life on the street and life at this, completely different, level. Still, I could not begrudge the partygoers their enjoyment, and I paused for a while tapping my foot to the band, which was belting out an incessant beat of what seemed to me to be a collection of gypsy or traditional Romanian folk songs. There were two accordions, a couple of trumpets, or perhaps they were cornets, a trombone and a guitar, all combining into an urgent and exciting cacophony which was strangely exhilarating. There was a singer, but the noise of the band almost drowned him out, notwithstanding the presence of a microphone which appeared glued to his mouth. All the men I saw appeared to be uniformly dressed in waistcoats of varying colours and tie-less shirts, in various stages of sweaty celebration, and all seemed to be having a wonderful time.

What a contrast with what I was about.

Above the noise, I was just able to make myself heard at the reception desk. My pocket dictionary gave me a basic translation of 'nurse', and without the faintest idea of how I should pronounce my question, I yelled "Assistenta Anglia?" Given that I looked hopelessly out of place, and, no doubt, very Western rather than Eastern, the receptionist didn't need to guess very hard as to my enquiry.

Probably because of the deafening music, any failure in my pronunciation appeared to have made little difference, because she pointed at the ceiling with one hand, and the number of the room with the other, gesturing towards the rows of numbered hooks and pigeonholes behind her.

Making my way upstairs to the second floor, I found the room, and knocked.

"Intra," said a female voice, and I went in to find two young women and a young man sitting in small easy chairs around the remainder of a meal on a coffee table in the middle of the room. They looked at me enquiringly.

I haltingly introduced myself and dropped my rucksack on the floor.

"I was told that you were here, volunteering your help to the orphanages."

"That's true," said one of them. "And…?"

"Well," I said, "I was in contact with Mary Gibson of the Romanian Orphanage Trust and she gave me your address. When I asked what I might bring across, I was told that supplies of Hibiscrub, E45 and Pholcodine linctus were desperately short, and so I've brought some with me in some modest attempt to be of some use… while I try to adopt a couple of children. Oh, and I was also asked to bring a couple of swimming pools."

I had, of course, got everything back to front and had

made a pretty awkward stab at explaining what I was about, but at least it set out my stall.

The nurses, bless them, focused immediately on my two offerings. "We need those desperately," said one of them, smiling. "Come and sit down and tell us what this is really about."

They introduced themselves. Liz, the oldest of the three, spoke with a soft Scottish accent. Anna, the younger of the two nurses, a blonde whose prettiness stood out against the drab surroundings, was clearly English. And then there was Dominic, a tall, slim young man who, like his room-mates, had persuaded their respective health authorities to allow the three of them, all with paediatric experience, to travel to Romania, without pay, to offer their services to the orphanages.

When I explained in rather clearer terms why I was there, their mood became sombre.

"The Romanians don't like it, you know," said Liz. "They won't co-operate with you, and they will make you feel pretty unwelcome."

I told them what had happened in Bacau and how I had been warned by one of their colleagues, Meg Bennett, of her own experience of Romanian antipathy. I didn't tell them quite how uneasy I felt when I was told to leave the town, but I wanted to make it clear that I was not going to give up at this early stage.

Like me, they had been appalled when pictures had first dribbled out of the country – why else would they have come? But I reflected that while they were bringing their skills into the country, here was I, unskilled in anything that could be remotely called useful, seeking to extract children from the same country.

"But our motives," I continued, "are the same. We are all desperately worried for the future of the children."

"Well, you're right, of course," said Anna. "But you'll get no help from them, and you must be ready to return to England empty handed."

"OK, but I've come all this way and I'm going to give it my best shot. Which is why I would appreciate some guidance from you."

"We can tell you what's going on, but you'll appreciate that we can't do anything more," said Liz. "Officially, we're guests of the Romanian government, such as it is. They're providing us with this accommodation, and basically they leave us to our own devices. If they suspected that we are actively co-operating with attempts to remove 'their' children, we'd be shown the door pretty quickly. And the children need as much help as we can possibly give them."

"I understand – so maybe you can just advise me where I might start?"

"Of course," said Anna, "but that's not that easy. You want to avoid Orphanage Number 5 – that's the Aids orphanage."

Oh, God. Could things get any worse for these kids? "How come there's an Aids orphanage?"

"It all came from tainted blood products," said Dominic. "The government – for which read Ceauşescu – allowed the importation of unchecked blood to hospitals from Africa when patients needed transfusions – and when those adults had children… bingo."

"And, of course, the orphanages aren't orphanages at all," I said.

Dominic agreed. "Ceauşescu outlawed contraception and abortion – and actively encouraged childbirth. What couldn't be produced by machinery or automation could be manufactured by an increase in the workforce – you know the Confucius saying: 'many hands make light work'? Ceauşescu went further. He wanted a 'people's army'. He even arranged tax breaks for families with children.

"If the children couldn't be supported, the parents could ask that they be placed in orphanages until their financial situation improved. Believe it or not, they could ask for the children's return when they felt that they could be productive."

I shook my head in bewilderment. "But there are tens of thousands of these children around the country. And there aren't tens of thousands of families waiting to welcome them back."

And somebody – it might have been Graham Prestridge – had told me that if a child reached the age of three and had not been reclaimed, they would be classed as an 'incurable' and removed to another state institution.

We sat in an uncomfortable silence.

Until Liz seemed to make up her mind. "We're going to Orphanage Number One tomorrow. We've not been there before, but I can give you the address. We don't really know what to expect, but then the whole situation is crazy. We might see you there."

Clutching the address and my now empty rucksack, I left them. Three good people facing a tsunami of grief. What could I possibly do which would even compare with their generosity?

FOURTEEN

"Men are generally more careful of the breed of their horses and dogs than of their children."

William Penn, *Reflexions and Maxims*, 1644–1718

I returned to Hotel Parc with my spirits pretty low. I trudged, rather than walked, my way back to the hotel, without any great enthusiasm. I now had the address of an orphanage, but the unenthusiastic messages from the front line were now reinforced by nurses with first-hand experience. I couldn't share this with my mother. When I got back to our room, she was already asleep and so I lay, in silence, wondering what the next day would hold.

And I was up before her, washed and ready to leave, by 8am.

I decided that I would take some, but not all of my remaining supplies. Two of the industrial-looking tubs of E45 cream, and one of the swimming pools seemed to fit the bill as much as anything else, and with them in my rucksack, I went back down through reception and out into the front of the hotel.

In fact, I was lucky enough to find a taxi driver, or rather the driver of a car with a taxi sign clinging precariously to its roof from which a family was disembarking into the hotel. I showed him the address that had been given to me by Liz, the night before, and he nodded and gestured me to get in.

As it turned out, it was not that far away and we arrived well before nine o'clock. But the question was, where was the orphanage? The driver had brought me to the right street but had no idea at all of the whereabouts of any orphanage and we had to agree to part on the corner of the street.

I got out and looked around me. I was on a wide road, with large turn-of-the-century buildings on either side, with broad pavements punctuated by a number of regularly spaced trees. There was no hint or sound of anything that could remotely be labelled orphanage.

I walked up and down the road for about a hundred yards without any clear idea of where I was, until, on the other side of the road, I saw a middle-aged professional-looking man in a short-sleeved shirt and slacks, carrying a briefcase, walking, I surmised, on his way to work. He was the only pedestrian I had seen in the last 15 minutes.

I went across to him and asked him if he spoke French. "Mais oui," he said, "un peu."

What a relief.

I had no idea, however, what the French word for orphanage was. Embarrassed, I found myself asking whether he had any idea of the location of the children's hospital.

He frowned. "Un hôpital? Pour enfants?"

Well, I said, a sort of hospital.

He paused and looked up and down the road. Apologetically, he said that the closest match he could think of was a building further down the road and round one of the corners. He pointed further back to where the taxi had gone. There was nothing more he could tell me and so I thanked him and he and I went on our separate ways.

The sun was already well over the rooftops and the day was starting to warm up, but I stayed in the relative cool of the shady side of the street and made my way round the corner which my informant had identified. And, sure enough, there, on the other side of the road, was a large building which looked as if it was about to fall down.

The building itself was festooned with scaffolding which was itself rusty and, in parts, looking as if it would fall apart. It might well, in earlier times, have been comparatively handsome in that there were two gateways leading to and from a large semicircular driveway but which was itself now pocked with holes and small valleys and, in parts, blocked by fallen scaffolding rods.

Between the gateways was a long low wall, into which were fixed railings, some 10 feet or so high, all of them revealing peeling paintwork and rust from top to bottom. Set to one side of each end of the fencing and the gateways were two large gate houses, themselves linked to the main building, but with doorways leading onto the drive.

In the middle of the semicircle there was rubble, broken bricks and more scaffolding poles, all heavily overgrown with weeds.

There was a dirty sign painted on a board midway along the fencing. It was so old and decrepit that it was virtually impossible to make out the writing, save that I did see one word that I could just make out and which I recognised. *Copii*.

Children.

I shouldered my rucksack and approached what I reckoned must be the orphanage. For no particular reason, I chose the right-hand gateway and, as I approached it, the door of the right-hand gatehouse opened and a fearsome-looking woman in a headscarf, dirty apron and floor-length skirt of indeterminate colour appeared. She folded her substantial forearms across her equally large stomach and glared at me.

"Da?" she demanded, more by way of a challenge than a question.

I decided that I would not let her face me down and I looked at her coolly, without breaking stride.

"Director?" I replied, as firmly as I could, gesturing vaguely towards the building, but making it plain that I wanted to find my way to the head of the establishment.

Discomforted by my self-assurance, the *babushka* retreated marginally and pointed to the corner of the building furthest from us both, where I could see a doorway under an apron of scaffolding.

"Multu mesc," I threw at her – a curious word which seemed to be part Latinate and part French. I had already heard a number of Romanians splicing French words into their conversations, such as 'Merci'. In any event, it seemed to satisfy her, and she turned on her heel and disappeared back into the darkness of her doorway.

Left to my own devices, I picked my way through the detritus and weeds and pushed through the doorway into an unlit corridor. Not knowing which way to turn, I chose left, and was just able to find my way to the end of the passage by the dim illumination which pierced the few grimy windows along one side of my route, breathing in the musty air, and kicking through scattered rubbish ahead of me.

There was even scaffolding inside the corridor, let alone outside the building, and loose plasterwork littered the floor. I could just make out holes of varying sizes both on the ceiling and the side walls from which the plaster was continuing to dribble.

At the very end of the corridor was a door without any sign or indication of what lay behind. It was not locked and I went through it and found myself in a cleaner hallway, with another door ahead and a door to my right-hand side. This door was open, and I found that it opened into a small office in which there were two dark-haired, rather attractive young women, in starched white figure-hugging uniforms, chatting to each other. There was a desk and a typewriter in the office, and I guessed that these figures were unlikely to be nurses and that they were probably masquerading as secretaries.

They turned to me enquiringly.

I decided to adopt the same strategy as with the gatekeeper.

"Director," I said, as imperiously as possible.

One of them, marginally prettier than the other, got up, pulled her skirt down to her knees and walked past me to the door at the end of the corridor, knocked, and went in. A moment later, not looking best pleased, she re-emerged, and beckoned me through.

I walked into a room which turned out to have all the appearance of a good-sized drawing room, with bay windows on two sides. It was dominated by a large partner's desk which was almost bare except for an incongruous-looking Sony radio and cassette player – something akin to an upmarket 'ghetto-blaster'.

To my left was a large bookcase, with artfully placed glossy magazines, and on shelving along the wall behind the desk was a coffee machine. The bay windows had seating and cushions, and in each of the bays were Liz, Anna and Dominic, my Romanian Orphanage Trust nursing acquaintances from the previous night, together with about six others, who I assumed were their colleagues, all dressed in their own nursing fatigues.

Facing them, behind the desk, was an imposing-looking man with aquiline features and a substantial shock of dark hair, greying at the temples, wearing a starched white coat, shirt and tie. And in the middle of the room was a young woman, again attired like the two in the office, looking extremely uncomfortable.

I assumed that I had managed to find my way to the Director's office, and he silently ushered me to a seat close to the door, where I sat and waited.

The scene was quite bizarre. Not only was the young woman in the middle of the room looking pretty uncomfortable, but so were all the British nurses. The Director seemed perfectly calm but appeared to wear a general air of puzzlement. Part of the reason became clear pretty quickly.

The young woman was doing her best to interpret from English into Romanian, but she was obviously struggling, bearing in mind that her grasp of the English language was close to zero. Clearly, none of the nurses spoke Romanian, and the Director most certainly did not speak English.

I had a brainwave.

"I wonder if I can help out by translating through French," I whispered to Liz.

"Anything," she said. "We're getting nowhere."

I turned to the Director. "Excusez-moi, Monsieur, mais, si vous parlez Français, on vous aide, si vous voulez. Je puis traduire de l'Anglais alors en Français."

He smiled, obviously relieved, and said something to the equally relieved-looking young woman, who promptly left the room.

I set about my task as best I could, introducing the nurses to the Director, whose name, I learned, was Ursuliano. The breast pocket of his white coat proclaimed that he was a doctor but I was soon to conclude that that was not an accurate description. However, for the time being, I did my best to act as interpreter, despite the difficulties that immediately presented themselves.

There was no difficulty with translation or language. The problem seemed to be that Ursuliano was wholly unready for the offers of help which the nurses were pressing upon him. They had told me the night before that this was their first visit to this particular orphanage and they were desperate to be of some use to the overstretched personnel.

Where could they apply themselves?

"Anywhere you want to," he replied, in French.

But where was the greatest need?

"I'm sure one of my assistants can show you around," he said.

A number of nurses clearly had specialist qualifications, some with disabilities, some with breathing disorders, and all with paediatrics. Could he suggest where they might make themselves the most useful?

He had no suggestions at all, and seemed wholly unaware both of the needs of the children within the orphanage and how any of the nurses might be able to help them.

I explained to Liz that I was not getting very far with him.

"I'm sorry," I said, "but I assure you that he is giving nothing away. I'm giving you the answers that he is giving me, and although they seem pretty empty, I don't know how or whether we're going to get any better information from him. It's most odd."

"I agree," said Liz, "but it seems that the most we can do we is get to work and do the best that we can, and find our own way around the orphanage."

And in due course, Ursuliano whistled up another assistant, who led the nurses out of the room, leaving the two of us together.

Quite apart from the curious exchanges in which I had become involved, the physical scene remained bizarre, if not shocking. I was sitting in a cool, nicely decorated drawing room, surrounded not by medical texts but by the comforts of a well-ordered study, while outside, I had already seen evidence of decay and abandonment.

"Voulez-vous un café?" volunteered the Director.

Certainly, I said, I would love one. He turned to his coffee machine and after a moment produced a small cup of bitter-tasting black liquid.

Now that the nurses had gone, he asked, after a moment, what I was doing there.

I took out the document which I had shown to Dr Sadovici in Bacau, my statement of intent or declaration, translated into Romanian back in England. Passing it to him, I sat back while he read it to himself.

When he had finished, he gave it back to me with a frown on his face. He did, he said, have a good number of children in the orphanage, but he very much doubted that any of them were available for adoption.

I listened to him in stunned silence. I knew that there must have been more than six hundred children in this orphanage and I simply could not believe my ears.

Anyway, he continued, he would call one of his assistants to take me around the orphanage just to see if a child was available. He pressed a buzzer on his desk, summoning his pretty 'secretary' into the room.

He spoke briefly to her, and after she had left, I decided to at least offer him the supplies which I had brought from the hotel. First, I took out the swimming pool which, in its boxed state, was easy enough to understand. He seemed vaguely pleased.

Then I took out the tub of E45 cream.

He looked at it, uncomprehendingly. Of course, on this tub, there was only English script and no illustrations as to the use or application of the substance, but I had imagined that any clinician would know immediately what it was, since the chemical formulae were clearly displayed on the lid.

Ursuliano unscrewed the lid and looked at the contents. His look of puzzlement was almost comical. Finally, before

I could prevent him, he dipped his forefinger into the cream, extracted a dollop, and put it straight in his mouth.

"Non, non," I said. "C'est médication pour les maux de peau. On me dit que les enfants souffrent de maux de peau entre les jambs." I was unsure how I could make it more graphic. All I could think of at that moment was sore legs. Anything more intimate was beyond my vocabulary.

Ursuliano replaced the lid and put the tub on his desk. He was about to thank me when there was a knock on the door, and a tired-looking youngish woman shuffled in. She too wore a white coat, although in rather less of a starched state. On her breast pocket was stencilled Doctor Zoitsanu.

I was puzzled as to just how many doctors frequented this establishment and suspected that, on the contrary, these titles were meaningless. However, Zoitsanu was able to communicate with me in French and, after a few words with Ursuliano, she indicated that she had been deputed to take me around the orphanage to see whether or not a child was 'available'.

I said goodbye to Ursuliano, who made it plain that he would very much like to see me again and I should call in once more to share a coffee with him. I promised that I would, and followed Zoitsanu into the corridor, where we found two rangy American women and a young Romanian man who was clearly acting as their interpreter.

I did not introduce myself to the Americans, who were very much tied up in their own conversation, but I spoke briefly to the interpreter who said that he had come over from America with them, having left Romania some five years before. In the brief moment I had to speak to him, he made it plain that he was not at all comfortable with the task he was now undertaking, and that he found the state of the building quite shocking.

The four of us moved off, following Zoitsanu down the corridor, avoiding the scaffolding poles as we did so. For her part, she trudged, with a noticeable limp. I caught up with her and asked if she was all right.

"J'ai eu la polio quand j'étais un enfant," she said. I made sympathetic noises and fell back, into our mournful crocodile.

We negotiated a maze of corridors, each one of them in a similar state of disrepair. I assumed that we were moving into the main part of the orphanage, not just from the number of corridors we negotiated, but because of the oppressive smell which assailed our nostrils. Everywhere we turned, there was a dreadful stink of human excrement. It was so bad that the initial onslaught almost made me gag, but I found, eventually, that the smell became part of the backdrop which my senses just had to, and eventually did, cope with.

Halfway along one corridor, I came across a window just above head height. I thought I saw misshapen arms of disabled children pressing up against the glass. Zoitsanu opened the door immediately next to the window but had barely got it ajar when it was shut very firmly in her face, accompanied by some sort of expletive from inside the room. She looked around, embarrassed. The Americans were still deep in conversation. The interpreter and I shared a look of surprise but said nothing.

Zoitsanu led on.

More corridors, more twists and turns, more rubble and more scaffolding, until we came to another door, this one leading into the open air. Zoitsanu ushered us through, on to an open area about the size of a tennis court. My immediate impression was of baked earth and occasional tussocks of grass. In the middle of the area was some sort of rusted contraption which might have been an intricate seesaw that had long since collapsed. There was a bedraggled tree and a small swing with no seat.

This appeared to be some sort of backyard, entirely surrounded by high walls, three of which were the walls of the orphanage itself, the other a wall of about 15 feet in height. In the corner furthest from us sat two forlorn-looking orderlies in scruffy white uniforms, smoking.

And coming towards us, some stumbling, some crawling, and some managing to run, twenty-five or so infants, those who were able to walk, with their arms raised towards us.

The scene was utterly desperate. The children were not begging. Rather they were imploring us to pick them up. I knelt down on one knee in the dust and was immediately festooned by a heap of filthy children. One, perhaps a little stronger than the rest, climbed onto my arm and surveyed me solemnly.

I became almost detached from the scene, observing myself and the American women, who were wandering around the yard with a video camera making inane and thoughtless comments. Over the heads of the children, I saw the interpreter turn on his heels and leave by the one door through which we had come. The orderlies did not react at all and simply sat and continued smoking. For her part, Zoitsanu hovered around the outskirts of the throng of children.

Kneeling there, I had no idea what was going on. The yard was hot and oppressive, without any hint of fresh air. The children were dressed in a variety of tiny sweatshirts, baby-grows and vests, all terribly grubby and, without exception, smelling to high heaven. The variety of slogans and designs on a number of the vests made it pretty obvious that the children were dressed in clothes which had been donated from across Europe. How long each of them had worn their particular trophy was open to question, but it was pretty clear that there was no such thing as a laundry.

Growing stiff, I got to my feet. The little boy who had clambered on to me right at the start was still clamped to my arm.

Zoitsanu came over to me. "Aimez-vous lui?"

In fact, he was quite a handsome little chap, still looking at me, with a half-smile on his lips. Unusually for this part of the world, he had fair hair, with remarkably long eyelashes.

"Que s'appelle-t-il?" I asked.

"Ticci," she replied, her pronunciation making the name sound like 'Titch'.

Sensing that I approved of the little boy, she motioned me to put him down and follow her out of the yard. We would have to speak to 'the social worker', she explained. Bemused, I followed her, leaving the Americans to their chatter as they continued to wander around the yard, filming.

As we left the yard, one little boy, rather taller than the rest, and clearly able to walk faster than the others, scampered over to us, and stood wailing by the door. He had red tightly curled hair and a very marked divergent squint, and, like all the others, was covered in dust and dirt. His distress was palpable and quite shocking. I stood for a moment, desperate to find some way to comfort him, but feeling totally powerless.

Zoitsanu beckoned impatiently, and I turned away, but with a dreadful sense that I was abandoning the poor child all over again.

I did my best to concentrate on Zoitsanu, who led me with her shambling gait back through the corridors and to the front of the orphanage. We walked out into the open air once more, and over the potholed driveway to the gatehouse on our right, opposite the lair of the *babushka*. I followed her into what turned out to be an office, where at that moment there was just one occupant, a well-dressed woman, heavily made-up, and with a substantial head of permed red hair.

Zoitsanu went straight over to her and began talking, while I stood in the doorway, unsure where to put myself.

The conversation between Zoitsanu and the woman, whom I took to be the social worker, began very quickly to get out of control. I was able to detect that the social worker was becoming more and more angry with Zoitsanu, who, ultimately, retreating from the onslaught, came over to me with a hangdog expression on her face.

"I'm very sorry," she said in French, "but that child is not available for adoption."

Bewildered, I remained silent, not knowing quite what to say.

There was a further exchange between Zoitsanu and the social worker.

"But," she said, turning back to me once more, "there is one child who is available."

"Yes?" I said.

"Il s'appelle Petre George. Avez-vous lui rencontré?"

What on earth did she mean? Of course I hadn't met him. I didn't have the faintest idea what she was talking about or who she was referring to. I would have thought that that was pretty obvious, but then again, the situation was becoming more surreal by the minute.

Zoitsanu cast something of a fearful look over her shoulder at the social worker before turning back to me.

Would I like to meet him, she asked?

Certainly, I said, and so we retraced our steps once more through the foul-smelling corridors and eventually to the same backyard.

The scene was just as before, save that the American women had disappeared. The orderlies were still smoking and, as we came through the door, the children again did their best to rush towards us. Once more I found myself surrounded, although this time I remained standing, wondering what would happen next.

Zoitsanu went over to the orderlies, chatting to them, seeking, I assumed, to identify the one child of whom she had spoken. Reluctantly, one of them got up and carefully put her cigarette on the bench before coming across to the group of children milling around me.

At the very edge of the group, she picked up one of the weaker-looking children, who had been either too slow to keep up with the others or had been shouldered aside by the stronger infants, and, pushing her way through the throng, she handed him to me.

I put him on the crook of my arm and did my best to examine this offering who was wearing a stained and grubby vest which was rather too big for him. Like the other children, he had no shoes.

Unusually, his head was not shaved to the skull like many of the other children. Instead, he had long dark hair which was plastered over his forehead. His head tended to loll forward, and I was quite unable to engage him with any eye contact, even while moving the forefinger of my free hand in front of his face. There was no reaction at all.

His face had a deathly pallor, while from his nose, two green parallel lines of thick green mucus moved down from his nostrils, across his mouth and onto his chin. He had painful-looking red spots on his cheeks and neck, and, as far as I could see, many more on his arms and legs.

He made no sound whatsoever. I, for my part, found it impossible to engage him in any way, even to the extent that clicking my fingers close to each of his ears produced no perceptible response.

Indeed, the only outward sign of life, other than that his eyes remained open, was a warm trickle down my forearm as he urinated, soaking both my arm and the side of my T-shirt before I realised what was happening.

Zoitsanu came up to me.

"Ça suffit?" she said.

What on earth did she mean by that? Certainly I had had enough experiences that morning to last a lifetime, but that wasn't the point. Had she meant to translate something rather different from Romanian? Did she intend to ask whether I was satisfied?

Struggling to make sense of the situation, I thought back to David Rapley, the family GP at his surgery in leafy Warwickshire. What was it he had said? "Try," he had told me, "to find a child no older than 18 months."

I looked from the child to Zoitsanu and back again.

"Quel âge a-t-il?"

She looked at us both. "Il a presque deux ans." An assertion which later proved to be palpably false.

Really? He could have been any age to my untutored eyes, but at least the addition of 'almost' seemed to be roughly within the parameters set by David.

"Voulez-vous lui prendre?" she said.

Does time ever stand still? Certainly, in my experience, it speeds up and slows down at the most inappropriate times. Now, however, it slowed down to freeze-frame pace.

I could feel the sun on my back, burning my neck and sucking the air out of this dreadful place. The yard was eerily silent and, apart from the shuffling children, there didn't seem to be any sign of life. The orderlies were taking no interest in the scene at all, and Zoitsanu simply stood in front of me, squinting against the sun and waiting for my answer.

What on earth was I committing to? Where was the nearest paediatrician? Was this child disabled? He was not responding in any way to any of my endeavours, which might suggest some sort of neurological deficit or that he was deaf. I was not even sure that he could walk properly.

Did he have Aids? How old, in fact, was he, given that it was quite unlikely that Zoitsanu had any information on him at all? Could anyone give me an objective medical or clinical opinion? This little scrap of humanity appeared to be in a perfectly dreadful state, but the extent of his difficulties was wholly beyond any assessment that I could bring to bear at that moment.

His head drooped down to his chest as he wobbled slightly on my arm.

I looked back at Zoitsanu.

She stared first at me and then at the yard. There was the vaguest hint of a sneer on her face – or was she as uncomfortable as I was?

Again she asked me in her formulaic French. "Will he do?"

Again the silence.

Dear God in heaven, what was wrong with the world? Could no one help me?

I had to snap out of this. I glanced once more at the child and then looked straight at Zoitsanu.

"Bien sûr."

Of course.

FIFTEEN

"I never wonder to see men wicked, but I often wonder
to see them not ashamed."

Swift, *Thoughts on Various Subjects*, 1711

Zoitsanu displayed no emotion. She gestured to me
to put the child back on the ground and leave him.
I put him down on the baked earth as gently as
possible and watched him stumble slowly away. He fell
down almost immediately but picked himself up without
too much difficulty as I looked back, following Zoitsanu
through the doorway.

"On doit encore visiter le bureau," she said, looking
extremely miserable at the prospect of coming face-to-
face with the social worker again. Still, that appeared to be
obligatory, and so we returned to the office where we were
confronted once more.

The social worker could not speak French, and
everything then had to be conducted through Zoitsanu,
who appeared to be something of a reluctant interpreter.

I knew that I needed the consent of the parents if I was to
progress to the next stage, and I asked Zoitsanu to find out
what the social worker knew of the child's mother and father.

The social worker regarded me coldly, while Zoitsanu stumbled through her interpreting. It appeared that the child's father was unknown. The social worker did, however, know the whereabouts of the mother.

Did I have a lawyer, the social worker demanded, with a look of disdain on her face. Certainly, I looked something of a sight, my hitherto clean T-shirt now stained with infant urine, and my trousers scuffed and dirty from my kneeling in the backyard.

"Non," I replied to Zoitsanu. "Je suis avocat moi-même."

She raised her eyebrows momentarily, whether from surprise or disbelief, and imparted my declaration to the social worker, who made it plain that that was not the response that she was expecting, nor one that she liked very much.

I had, of course, been warned about the probability of corrupt lawyers and the passing of money, and I sensed that the social worker was herself perfectly prepared to accept a bribe and indeed probably expected it. However, she would be getting nothing from me, and any sort of referral fee or the like to a dubious lawyer was clearly out of the question. I was obviously not a welcome prospect.

She spoke once more to Zoitsanu, whose halting translation provided me with an outline, albeit reluctant, of the next steps which were to be taken. Today was Thursday, and, the social worker asserted, she would ensure that the mother would come to the orphanage on the following Monday and would sign the necessary forms of consent to enable me to adopt the child.

Zoitsanu assured me that there would be no problem and ushered me out of the office, looking mightily relieved that the meeting was over.

I thanked the social worker over my shoulder as we left, but received no response. I wondered if I should hand over some of the comforts which I had brought from England next time I saw her, in an endeavour to secure her co-operation. There was no one I could ask but I decided to have something in reserve for the following Monday when I was to return.

Back once more in the heat of midday, I decided that the best thing I could do would be to go back to the hotel and clean up, and report to my mother as to what had happened. But no sooner did I get to the entrance than I found the Americans' interpreter standing by the far gate, smoking and looking thoroughly upset. I went across to him.

"You know," he said immediately, "I left this country five years ago, and it was in a pretty god-awful state then. Now look at it. I had absolutely no idea what I had let myself in for when I agreed to come over with those Americans. I have never seen children so badly treated and I am ashamed of Romania. The sooner I can get back to the States, the better."

"What did those women think they were doing?" I asked.

"Do you know," he said, "I'm not sure that even they know. I guess that they thought they might take pictures of a cuddly little baby or two, and choose one to take back to America with them. Now it's wake-up time. I'm Romanian and even I wasn't ready for what we've seen here today, so I can't imagine what is going through their minds."

"Well," I said, "the Director claimed that no children at all are available for adoption from this orphanage, although, to be frank, I don't believe him. I sense that children may well be available but only on payment of money. It wouldn't make sense otherwise. Why take me and those two women around the orphanage if no children would be made available?"

He sucked on his cigarette. "I'm not going back in. It's a dreadful place and it makes me feel ill just to look at the children and to see the state that they are kept in. And the smell!" He pulled a face to emphasise his disgust.

"That's exactly why I'm here," I said. "Television pictures in England, and presumably round the world, have shown the state of these places, and I know that I'm not alone in my attempt to get one or more children out of here. In fact, my local social services have approved my attempts to take two children back to England and somehow I must find another."

He said nothing, looking into the middle distance.

I chanced my arm. "I don't suppose you would be very kind and take me to another of the orphanages here to see whether or not I can find another child? I've been given the address of Orphanage Number Two, and that is my obvious next port of call."

He looked at me doubtfully. He appeared to weigh up the alternatives. Stay outside or go back into that ghastly building. And if he was to stay outside, maybe he could give me a lift. After a moment, he dropped his cigarette and ground it out in the dust.

"I'll tell you what. I'll drive you to the second orphanage and drop you outside. But please don't ask me to go in."

"Deal," I said. "That really is very kind of you."

His car was parked on the road outside, and despite his absence from Bucharest for the last five years or so, it didn't take more than a few minutes for him to find his bearings and then to find Orphanage Number Two, which appeared to be the other side of the city.

We drove to a run-down area, with a good number of demolished buildings. And there, at the end of what appeared to be a cul-de-sac, I saw high rickety gates, fashioned out of chicken wire, affording access down a dusty roadway to what was obviously my destination.

My Romanian/American helper dropped me on the main road and said that he really would rather not go anywhere near the orphanage.

"I hope you understand," he said. "This has been a really upsetting experience for me and I want to avoid repeating it."

I thanked him and shook his hand warmly. "You've been very kind," I said, "and without you, I certainly wouldn't have been able to find my way here easily or even at all."

He wished me luck and drove in a wide circle, back in the direction from which we'd come, leaving me standing on the corner, wondering what on earth I was in for next.

What I did know from my meeting with Liz and the others at Hotel Lido was that the Director of Orphanage Number Two was a woman who either spoke French or even possibly was French, so I picked up my now empty rucksack and walked into the grounds of the orphanage.

I realised that I had never asked the name of my helper.

***

The contrast with Orphanage Number One was marked. All around me, the ground seemed dark, almost black, the flattened earth of the area almost indistinguishable from the tarred surface of the road. As I walked down the road, I found myself between high chicken-wire fences, approaching what seemed to be a long, raised single-storey wooden building with a veranda along the length of one side. As I got closer, I could see a small group of nurses, perhaps four or five of them, sitting talking and looking over at children who were playing on ground on the other side of the chicken wire. Just like the backyard of Orphanage Number One, there were no facilities and little grass. The ground was dusty and beaten flat, and the children appeared to have nothing to play with save for the occasional tree stump. The ones I could see were doing little more than wandering aimlessly around or sitting on the ground.

I went up to the veranda and was about to announce myself in French when the nearest nurse to me spoke up.

"Hello," she said, "can I help you?"

"Hey," I replied, "you're English!"

"Well, no, actually, I'm from Aberdeen," she said, "but don't worry."

I explained that I had rather hoped that I could see the Director, having come away from Orphanage Number One and keen to continue to establish whether or not I could adopt another child.

"I'm sorry," she said, "but the Director is on holiday, and won't be back for a couple of weeks."

She came down the steps of the veranda and joined me as I looked around the barren surroundings.

"I and my friends have taken time off from our summer vacations to come and help here," she said. "And as you can see, the orphanages are in something of a state."

"To be honest," I said, "I really didn't know what to expect, but it's all pretty shocking. And that's why I'm here with my mother, endeavouring to adopt a couple of children."

As we walked, she told me that I wouldn't be successful in seeking any children from this particular orphanage but that I should be happy for these kids.

"Look," she said, "I can tell you where each of the children you see on that playground is going." As she pointed, she told me of their various destinations.

"That one is going to Germany. That little girl is off to Israel. That child to Canada. That one to South Africa…"

She paused, looking quizzically at me, for I was only half listening to her. I was watching a little boy who had fallen flat on his face and who had quite clearly hurt himself. But as I watched, he was picking himself up and wiping down his already dirty clothes.

I could not quite put my finger on it, but something was wrong.

She followed my gaze. After a moment, she said "You're wondering why he isn't crying, aren't you?"

I nodded.

"Crying, you know, is a natural reflex of an infant who is seeking comfort. But these children have long since learned not to cry. They learn from a very early age that crying simply wastes energy."

"So they don't cry?" I said weakly.

"That's right," she said. She looked me over.

"Because…" she said softly, as if to emphasise her words, "… nobody comes."

SIXTEEN

"There exist some evils so terrible and some misfortunes
so horrible that we dare not think of them, whilst their
very aspect makes us shudder; but if they happen to
fall on us, we find ourselves stronger than we imagined;
we grapple with our ill luck, and behave better than we
expected we should."

La Bruyère, *'Of Mankind', Characters*, 1688

I felt numb. In my struggle to keep hold of my thoughts,
I swore silently to myself, over and over again. Now
I remembered that in the backyard in Orphanage
Number One something had been missing which I had
overlooked. None of the children had made a sound, even
when scrambling towards us, except for that one red-head-
ed youngster who wailed uncontrollably as I left.

Nor were the children in this drab playground at Orphanage Number Two screaming with pleasure or indeed
any of the emotions that usually accompany children who
are running around, free to enjoy themselves. None of the
noises that I could associate with pleasure or distress existed.

I didn't know what to say. Indeed, there was nothing
I could say. I found it difficult to look this kind young

woman in the face. I was so unready for what she had told me that I felt unable, physically, to control my vocal cords. I feared that if I tried to say anything, I would choke, or that I might just manage a squeak.

I made a great effort to look around me, pretending to look at all the children, trying to regain some self-control, but I felt that I had to get away from the scene. Struggling to hide my distress, I thanked her more curtly than I should, and retreated, walking as quickly as I could back down the roadway and towards the gates.

And there between the tall chicken-wire fences I stood, weeping, hoping that I could not be seen but not caring if I was.

***

I had to get back to the hotel, partly to recover and partly to report back to my mother. My head was swimming, and I needed to get my bearings, emotionally.

I wiped my face, and made an effort to pull myself together, and walked away from Orphanage Number Two, into the traffic. I had absolutely no idea where I was, but I was clearly in a substantial built-up area, and I could see bus stops on either side of the road. Adopting the same tactic as a few nights before, I approached the queue at the nearest stop and again asked the one word, "Centru?" A young couple, clearly amused by my appearance and my limited use of the language, smiled and beckoned me onto a bus which was approaching at that moment.

The young man spoke English. "Here," he said, "you can

use this ticket," proffering what appeared to be the final part of what had been a stub of daily tickets or passes. "Hand it in if the collector comes round."

What a relief. I had no idea how to buy a ticket, let alone how much it might cost, and the simple and disarming generosity of this young man was something of a tonic.

He and his partner got off the bus before I did and, as he passed me, he said that the city centre was a few more stops down the road, so I stayed on board, disembarking with the bulk of the passengers at my destination. It was then a question of walking back to Hotel Parc, which I decided was better than hitching a ride. I needed to clear my head and make sense of the morning's events.

***

So, I had visited two orphanages and discovered one child out of many hundreds. It was dawning on me that I had no idea what I had let myself in for. Where had the boy come from? What was his state of health? Was he disabled? How old was he? He was clearly not an orphan, because the social worker spoke of his mother, so how come he was in the orphanage at all? Were any of the children in that dreadful place orphans? Now that I had visited two orphanages, there were probably two more in Bucharest which I could visit before having to go outside the city, but it struck me that any further expedition might cause difficulty with my attempts to sort out the arrangements for the child whom I had already found. These questions and many more swam around my head as I made my way back to the hotel.

When, an hour later, I got back to our room, I still had no answers.

"Well," I said, "I've found a child. But Orphanage Number One insists that there are no other children there who are available for adoption, and my visit to Orphanage Number Two produced a similar answer."

My mother seemed more optimistic than I felt, but mercifully she hadn't been exposed to some of the things that I had seen. "You've at least made a wonderful start," she said. "The question now is where we go from here."

And that indeed was the question, given that my mother did not appear terribly well. I had already noticed her shortness of breath and her difficulty in getting about, but now she seemed to be in increasing distress.

"Are you quite alright?" I asked. "You don't look at the top of your game."

"I think I've got something of a tummy upset," she said, "possibly because of my silliness in taking some of the water in Bacau. But don't worry, I'll be all right. Why don't you get cleaned up and we'll go back to the orphanage this afternoon and you can show me this little boy."

So I stripped off and got back under the shower which, for all its inadequacies, allowed me to clean up and get rid of the dust and the smell of urine, so that, fifteen minutes later, I was refreshed, although given the summer heat and the time of day, I immediately began perspiring once more.

"Tell you what," I said, "let's get hold of a taxi or a lift, since I know where the orphanage is now, and I'll show you round."

So, as nonchalantly as a native, I managed to flag down a car just outside the hotel, and, for a dollar, the driver happily took us, under my guidance by way of pointing and nudging, to the gates of the orphanage.

I took my mother by the arm, and shepherded her through the gateway furthest from the *babushka*. To my left the social worker's office door was shut, and although the door to the opposite gatehouse was open, the custodian did not put in an appearance.

I held onto my mother. "Watch where you are walking, Ma. You have to look up and sideways because of the scaffolding, and also where you are putting your feet, because of the rubble."

We passed in through the door to the orphanage and, as before, I turned left, making my way to the Director's office. The secretaries' door was ajar, and I knocked.

"Direktor, va rog," I said, rather more politely than earlier that day.

She recognised me and displayed neither pleasure nor disdain but simply walked past us both and knocked on Ursuliano's door.

The sound of his deep voice, "Intra."

The secretary made way for us and in we went, once more into this room of stark contrast to the orphanage itself.

He recognised me immediately, smiling broadly. "Bienvenue."

I introduced my mother, who seemed very taken by this tall, imposing and hawkishly handsome man. Within moments, she, a better linguist than I, was chatting away with Ursuliano in French. For a moment or two, I left them to it but when, for a second, they ran out of steam, I interrupted, telling Ursuliano that a child had been found who was free for adoption.

He raised his eyebrows, but made no comment.

I asked him if he would be kind enough to summon Zoitsanu so that I could take my mother to see the child.

"Mais certainement," said Ursuliano, moving to the buzzer on his desk, summoning one of his secretaries. Whatever her typing skills, it didn't take her long to find Zoitsanu and, moments later, she appeared in the doorway.

"C'est après dejeuner, et les enfants se reposent," she retorted when I asked her if she would take us back to the yard. The children were no longer outside, she said, appearing to suggest that the children had had a meal and would be taking an afternoon nap.

Could I perhaps have my mother steal a look at him, nonetheless? Zoitsanu was not terribly enthusiastic but Ursuliano nodded and she led us out of his room, down the stinking corridors to another part of the orphanage. Made worse by the heat of the day, the smell was almost overpowering, and I saw my mother grab a handkerchief and put it over her nose. Once more, I had no idea where we were going, although I had heard Ursuliano use the term 'pavilion', both to the nurses that morning, and to Zoitsanu that afternoon. But as it turned out, however inappropriate the word, no description could possibly ready me for what we found.

Zoitsanu led us into a hallway which bisected two very large rooms, each of them almost the size of a tennis court.

On each side of the hallway was a partition, from the floor to waist height made up of either metal or wood, partly covered with flaking paintwork, and above that to the ceiling, of dirty glass.

On the other side of each partition I could see some of that which had been broadcast around the world. Row upon row of cots, jammed together, with just enough room for an orderly to walk up the middle of each room. The outside wall of each room was, from chest height, made up of windows, divided into little squares by rusting frames. Most of the glass, however, was missing. I was to realise, in the days to come, that the red spots which I could see on the exposed parts of all of the children were in fact mosquito bites. However badly nourished they were, they were an easy target for the hordes of hungry insects which descended on them through the broken windows, compounding their suffering in the hot summer nights.

In one corner of one of the rooms was a stone sink with one tap

High up at the end of the hallway was a television from which, bizarrely, came the sound of bagpipes. For some reason, there appeared to be some sort of documentary about Glasgow or Edinburgh, I knew not nor cared which, which was providing a surreal backdrop to this ghastly scene.

It was ghastly because in each of the cots was a child, in varying states of distress. This was not a calm or refreshing afternoon nap at all. The children might well have been fed, although how and with what I did not then know, but they were without exception terribly distressed. Cot after cot revealed a child swaying from side to side, seeking to comfort itself. Some were standing, gripping the bars of the cot, standing on one foot and then the other, others were flat on their back, rocking from side to side. Yet more were kneeling at the end of the cot, banging their head on the cot side.

The only sound came from the bagpipes.

I was ready for the smell and indeed now knew to expect silence. But yet again I was completely unready for what I saw.

There seemed to be only one orderly there, but Zoitsanu beckoned her over, and, pointing at me and my mother, appeared to ask where my foundling was located.

We were taken to the room on the left of the hall, and there, three-quarters of the way down one of the rows, I saw him. He was flat on his back and in great discomfort. He was just as frail as I remembered him from that morning, but now I saw that his stomach was distended, and his face was dark red. He was not making a sound but he was frowning terribly. Now and then he arched his back and went quite rigid, though whether in anger or pain I couldn't tell.

I felt utterly powerless to comfort him and didn't dare to pick him up. My mother, however, did pick him up and tried, unsuccessfully, to soothe him. He went rigid in her arms and threw himself backwards, and she barely managed to prevent him falling back into the cot.

"This," said my mother quietly, "is utterly appalling."

"Haven't you seen the TV pictures?" I asked her.

"Yes, but they simply don't convey the horror which we are looking at now."

I could only agree – even the television pictures were snatched, and could only give a two-dimensional and fleeting glimpse of the problems behind these walls. The broader sight of these poor children and the smell and the utter abandonment was quite overwhelming.

Looking back, despite the scenes being burned into my memory, none of them are in colour. Everything I saw within the two orphanages comes back in utter clarity, but in black and white.

I stroked the child's head, trying to comfort him, but it seemed to have no effect. His stomach was obviously causing him great discomfort, and he rocked his head from side to side, just as other children were rocking their whole bodies where they lay.

My mother and I decided to leave. I promised myself that I would return as often as possible and I asked Zoitsanu if that would be permitted.

She shrugged her shoulders. She supposed so.

Not feeling at all grateful for the way these poor children were being treated, I felt nonetheless that I should express some recognition for being able to see him, so, with a muttered "Merci," I guided my mother back through the corridors and into the open air. I flagged down another car – I was becoming an expert – and got us back to our hotel room, where my mother sank onto the bed.

She looked even more uncomfortable than she had when we had set off and I asked if she was okay.

"Frankly," she said, "whatever I have caught is getting worse."

As if to illustrate the point, she quickly went to the bathroom, where I could hear her throwing up.

When she reappeared, looking thoroughly exhausted, my worst fears seemed to be realised.

"I'm afraid that things are coming out of both ends," she said. "And although I'm letting you down, I really don't see how I can carry on here."

It was, in fact, quite plain that she was in a lot of trouble. She had not looked in the best shape at Heathrow airport. Now, looking at her in an attempt to appraise her state of health, it was pretty plain that she would be more of a hindrance than a help. Worse, she did appear to be in genuine distress.

"Look," I said. "I think the best thing for me to do is to get you on the first flight out of here back to London."

If I expected her to protest, she did not. To the contrary, she seemed relieved that she would be going home.

"It's not going to be terribly easy," I said, "but I'll find out where the airline office is and I'll see if I can bring your return flight forward.

She lay down, looking thoroughly miserable. "There's not much you can do this afternoon," she said, and indeed she was right . It was now well after four o'clock and I guessed that going back to the city centre, finding the airline office and negotiating a change of flight simply wouldn't fit into the remainder of the day.

"Okay," I said. "Try and stay as comfortable as you can tonight, and I'll get on with it first thing tomorrow morning."

She grimaced and went back to the toilet, where I was treated to the sound of more eruptions

Marvellous, I thought. Another step forward, two more steps back. And possibly worse. Clearly, my mother needed to get home and indeed wanted to leave as soon as possible. What could I do? Two priorities were jostling for my attention. Getting the little boy out of the orphanage, and getting my mother out of the country. In fact, I knew that there was not very much I could do about the orphanage, since the social worker had asserted that she was producing the mother on the following Monday. Therefore, I had to turn my full attention to getting to the airline office and sorting out my own mother's problem.

***

Next morning, Mircea told me where I could find the Tarom airline office. I worked out that it was very close to the city centre and, given that this was the coolest part of the day, I decided that at least on this first leg of my journey, I would walk into the city.

And the walk was pleasant enough, if, again, overwhelmingly dusty. The occasional heavy lorry rumbled past, spewing smoke and covered in dirt. How clean, I thought to myself, was UK traffic in comparison, something that I had never thought of until I arrived here. I marvelled, again, at the overwhelmingly grimy state of both the buildings and the traffic as, during my journey, I again started to pick up the taste of pollution in my mouth.

It was shortly before mid morning that I found myself in the centre, disorientated and unable to remember the directions Mircea had given me. But passers-by seemed perfectly content and indeed quite knowledgeable, when I approach them with the one question on my lips "Le bureau Tarom?"

They attempted to give me directions in Romanian, which went straight over my head, but their accompanying pointing and gesturing brought me closer and closer to my destination, until eventually, after a number of dead ends and misunderstandings, I found the Tarom office.

Inside the main door, I followed the signs, in Romanian and French, to the first floor of a substantial office building, and pushed my way into an open-plan office which was as close to a vision of Babel as I would ever wish to see.

The atmosphere was thick with cigarette smoke so dense that I could see layers of smoke drifting in thin horizontal lines from about head height up to the ceiling. The office was large – the equivalent, I suppose, of a decent-size booking hall – with about twelve desks, six or so on each side, placed in herringbone fashion along the length of the room.

Behind each desk sat what I assumed to be a booking clerk, with telephones, papers and volumes of timetables in front of him.

And around, over and seemingly on top of each desk was a swarm of gesticulating and shouting customers, all vying for attention and all speaking at once. I gave up counting how many people were in the room after it became clear that no desk had less than about twenty people around it.

There was absolutely no chance of my getting to any of the harassed-looking clerks. Not speaking Romanian, and without the non-queuing skills of the throng in front of me, I imagined that I simply wouldn't be able to get to the front, wherever that was, of any of the work stations set out before me.

This was no good at all, but what could I do? I surveyed the scene in increasing despair for a few minutes until I had a sudden brainwave. There was an alternative to competing with the teeming humanity in front of me: I should go to the airport.

So, finding my way downstairs once more, I was able, this being the city centre, to actually find a taxi. "Otopenei va rog," I said as I collapsed in the back, and wondered, as we headed away from the city, what on earth I would do if this didn't work.

It took about half an hour to reach the airport, where I paid off the taxi with what I felt to be a pitiful amount of lei, and made my way inside. The main terminal was almost deserted. I had no idea how many flights Otopenei would handle on a daily basis, but I guessed that there were not that many. Romania did not seem to me to be, as yet, a tourist destination of choice, and as far as I knew, none of the major European airlines counted it as one of their prime destinations.

But this meant that I was able, without much difficulty, to locate the Tarom office, where I found two middle-aged female clerks who seemed to have some time on their hands. There were no other members of the public around, and I was able to approach the office counter without clearing a path through a crowd of potential customers.

Thankfully, one of them spoke French, and almost immediately took to me. I told her that I and my mother had only arrived in Romania a week before, but that she was now suffering some sort of unpleasant stomach upset, and I needed to get her home.

She appeared to appreciate my concern for a sick parent and, from her nods and smiles, it was clear, too, that her colleague shared her sympathy.

They took my mother's ticket and pored over their flight schedules for a short time, until at last "Voila! Il y a un vol qui depart demain a dix heures pour Londres. Et je vous assure que j'ai trouvé un place pour votre maman."

I could have kissed her. She wanted no extra money and simply replaced the ticket with a fresh coupon, expressing her hope that my mother would recover as soon as possible after her return home. The two of them smiled broadly at me as I stuttered my thanks and left their office, found my way to the taxi rank, and took a cab back to Hotel Parc.

***

I told my mother the good news – good, that is, in that I had secured safe passage for her back home, but not so good if I was to succeed in my task for which the two of us had come here in the first place. However, she seemed relieved. Her condition, she said, had not improved since I left her, and indeed, if anything, she looked even more uncomfortable. However, she had somehow secured some bottled water, and at least she had the good sense not to allow herself to become dehydrated.

I decided that I couldn't simply sit around in our room while she went to and from the toilet, so I decided to revisit reception and maybe get something to eat.

Finding Mircea on duty, I went across to him. "Mircea, I think it would help if I could get hold of an interpreter." My experience with the social worker and, more recently, my sense of powerlessness at the Tarom city office, was making it pretty clear that I would struggle with officialdom even if, occasionally, I found a French speaker.

He thought for a moment. "I know someone who I think can help you. He is a friend who works at the Israeli embassy and I know that he has done some translating work in the past – and of course, not many Israelis speak Romanian! I'll try and get hold of him for you and see if he'll help. I'm back on duty tomorrow afternoon, and I might have some news then."

Great, I thought. Maybe that's one step forward again.

I decided to return to the dining room to see if there was anything to eat, and was met again by an empty room. The forlorn-looking waitress put in an appearance and, without prompting, placed some ham and tomatoes in front of me. I settled down to read the one book I had brought with me, *The Blind Watchmaker*. Not a good idea, for I was hardly in the mood for philosophy and I certainly wasn't ready for the aggressive atheism of Richard Dawkins. No doubt the emotional rollercoaster of the last couple of days had weakened my powers of reasoning, but as I struggled through the first chapters I found myself disagreeing with Dawkins at every turn. And the more he thumped the pages with his certainty that there is no god, the more I took it that the miracle of life, human or otherwise, could only be the gift of a deity. My struggle was not with that belief, but with my attempts to understand how there could be so much cruelty in the world in the face of a benign creator.

I remembered a sermon at Coventry Cathedral not many years before when the preacher, a survivor of the horrors of Auschwitz, recounted how one of the victims, facing death, plucked at the sleeve of a priest, also a prisoner.

"Where is your Jesus now?"

"My son," the priest had replied, "He is there, next to you in the line for the gas chamber. Do you not see Him? He is dying again for you and me – for us all."

Not an easy answer to digest, I thought at the time, moving though the imagery was. Now, I wondered to myself, where was Jesus in Orphanages One and Two? I knew that the answer was out there somewhere and was certainly not in the pages of *The Blind Watchmaker*, which I turned ever more slowly, until eventually I put it down, exasperated.

After staring into space for a while, I moved out into the hotel lobby, where there were a couple of free seats, deciding to watch the ebb and flow of arriving and departing guests. In the immediate reception area there appeared to be a flock of clerics, all dressed in long black coats, some with wide-brimmed black hats and some with skullcaps. I initially assumed that they were some sort of Orthodox order, although the majority language appeared to be heavily accented English. Perhaps they were Jewish?

They milled around the reception desk struggling, it seemed, to make themselves understood and it was clear that my friend Mircea was nowhere to be seen. There was another young man on duty and I knew that he understood a smattering of English, but it was quite plain that he had not taken to this group, and he was making no effort to converse with them in English or indeed in any language other than Romanian.

I watched them, fascinated, knowing that I should not really have been amused, when there was a sudden uproar from the public toilet. One of the larger clerics burst through the door, clutching what appeared to be two substantial wads of currency. However, it did not take long to realise that what he had in his hands were tightly packed pieces of paper with one or perhaps two valid 100 lei bills at each end. He had clearly been hoodwinked by a black marketeer into believing that he was exchanging what I assumed to have been a good number of dollars for an even greater number of lei.

"I've been robbed," he shouted in heavily accented English. "Call the police. This hotel is harbouring criminals!"

Everyone stopped what they were doing and looked across at him. There was a momentary silence, broken by the victim yelling, "There he is! Stop him! He is a thief! He has defrauded me!"

At that moment, the receptionist suddenly rediscovered his ability to speak English.

"What do you mean, thief?" he demanded. "And exactly what are you accusing this hotel of?"

The cleric looked at him, angrily. He shook his bundles of paper in his face.

"What do you think these are?"

"They look like pieces of paper to me," said the young man, remarkably calmly.

"Exactly!" said the cleric, triumphantly.

"And?" asked the receptionist. "What are you going to say to the police if they should come? That you were trying to buy currency on the black market?"

The cleric stood in front of him, his mouth opening and shutting in silence, struggling to contain himself. The conflicting emotions crossing his face were all too plain to see and I felt quite sorry for him, just as I had grudging respect for the unerring logic shown by the receptionist, who was for the moment managing to keep a straight face.

Eventually, stuffing the worthless paper into a large shoulder bag, the cleric turned on his heel and walked off. The receptionist shrugged his shoulders with a wry smile. In the confusion, the black marketeer had silently made good his escape.

Anyway, this Friday night, time for bed. I had to get my mother off to the airport the next day and then regroup. Hopefully, I would be visiting the orphanage and perhaps also I might somehow manage to get hold of an interpreter.

SEVENTEEN

"Beyond a certain pitch of suffering, men are overcome by a kind of ghostly indifference."

Victor Hugo, *Les Misérables*, 1865

In fact, the next day, while my mother seemed not to be in such bad shape, it was reasonably clear that she had lost all enthusiasm for Romania in general and our expedition in particular, and although there was no suggestion that we had to be at the airport more than an hour before the flight, I made sure that I had secured a taxi and we had departed from the hotel by eight o'clock.

I took her through to the departure hall and kissed her goodbye. "I'll let you know how I get on, and maybe, if you're fully recovered, you can pick us up from the airport and drive us home, assuming, that is, I ever make it out of here with any child."

"You know you will," she said, smiling weakly. "I'm terribly sorry I've let you down and I suppose we'll just have to make the best of it."

The irony of her use of "we" was lost on her, but I didn't think it was fair to point it out, and I simply handed over her suitcase and watched her as she went through the departure gate.

I thought that I should perhaps stick around until I saw the plane take off, just in case yet another mishap befell us, and so I wandered round the departure hall, looking blankly around, killing time until I heard the engines of the plane readying for take-off.

Satisfied that I now only had myself to look after, I found a taxi and decided to go first to the hotel and then perhaps walk to Orphanage Number One to see if I could see the child and even make myself useful in some capacity. I wanted to pick up some of the supplies I had brought to Romania to give to the orphanage staff, in the hope that that would keep me, at least to an extent, in their good books and that this might, somehow, permeate down to their care of the little boy. Back in my room, I loaded up a few tubes of toothpaste, some bars of soap, and yet another 200 pack of Kent into my rucksack, and made my way down to reception. Mircea, however, was not there, and I remembered that he had said he would be on duty in the afternoon, so I strolled out of the hotel and walked on to the orphanage.

***

When I reached Orphanage Number One once more, the social worker's office was again locked up, presumably because this was a weekend. I saw the *babushka* appear in the doorway of her gatehouse, but I didn't break stride and simply waved a brief greeting to her. She looked dolefully at me but did not come out and simply watched me as I went through to the orphanage door.

Out of courtesy, let alone necessity, I felt I ought to make my presence known to Ursuliano, and I went straight to his door and knocked

"Intra," again.

In fact, he was not alone. There was a young man, casually dressed, sitting in one of the bay windows, who seemed friendly enough, but at the same time vaguely sinister. Initially, I could not put my finger on the sense of unease that I felt, until I realised that he had exactly the same look about him as the men whom I suspected were members of the Securitate in Bacau.

"Voulez-vous prendre un café?" asked Ursuliano.

"Vous êtes tres gentil," I replied, "mais pas a ce moment, merci."

I explained that I would very much appreciate being allowed to go back to the pavilion to see the child and perhaps make myself useful.

"OK," said Ursuliano, and he immediately summoned an assistant whom I had not seen before, and instructed her, I assumed, to take me back into the main orphanage, which she did in complete silence. I thanked Ursuliano and promised that I would call to see him again in days to come.

It turned out that it was now feeding time for the children. I could not dignify what happened next with the description of lunch or indeed of anything remotely civilised, and what I saw left me feeling profoundly shocked.

There now appeared to be two orderlies shouldering the task of giving the children their midday meal. They went about their task with brutal efficiency, devoting just a moment's attention to each cot. When it came to my foundling's turn, the orderly produced a bottle with some horrible-looking gruel in it. I wondered how on earth the liquid could pass from the bottle to the child, until I realised that the hole in the teat had been artificially enlarged before being thrust into the infant's mouth. He was lying on his back, and the orderly simply stuck the bottle into his face, thrusting the teat into his mouth, and holding it vertically while the liquid gushed into his throat.

As it passed, and as the bottle emptied, I saw his little stomach distend once more, and I saw how distressed and angry he became, his face reddening and his eyes closing tight together as he frowned and struggled with the onslaught.

The orderly simply stood there, holding the bottle upright until it had emptied, which, given the enlarged hole, seemed to take only moments.

It was now pretty obvious why the boy had been in such discomfort when I saw him the previous day, but I was quite powerless to do anything about it. I simply looked numbly at the scene, before turning back to try and offer my assistance, to someone, anyone.

But what could I offer? I had no medical qualifications, and it was perfectly plain that I was not offering my services as a plasterer or the like. I was simply a T-shirted individual with no obvious qualifications, making pretty senseless offers of help with the task, if it were to be measured, of doing something to physically shore up the orphanage, or somehow help to provide nurture and care for the children.

I found an orderly and tried to explain that I was prepared to do whatever job, however menial, that might provide some support to the staff, even if it wouldn't immediately improve the lives of the children.

I offered her some of my supplies, some toothpaste, soap, and cigarettes, and tried to explain myself. She took my offerings almost furtively, but at the same time, in broken French, she made it clear that while she was almost overwhelmed by what she saw as my generosity, there was nothing I could do, and that perhaps I might like to return the next day outside feeding hours to be with the boy.

I felt utterly powerless. Powerless to do anything to help, powerless to protect the child from what I felt to be abuse. But grateful for small mercies, I decided that I would indeed come back the following day and I found my way out of the orphanage, out of that awful smell, and back to the surrounding roads. Dusty and dirty they might be, but they did not match the filth of the orphanage.

**

I remembered that there was a large park at one end of the long road that I had taken into Bucharest on my first walk into the city, and I decided to investigate and see whether I could at least relax in halfway decent surroundings. And, in fact, the park turned out to be delightful, with an enormous lake, trees, and walkways within long grassy avenues. I settled down by the lake and stretched out in the sun, listening to the chatter of families and the screams and giggles of little children as they scampered around their parents.

But it was not a happy experience. I raised myself on one elbow and looked around me. Within a stone's throw were a couple of families sitting and playing with their children in a scene of utter normality. Infants were toddling around, being followed closely by one or other parent, who lifted them into the air from time to time, while they screamed in delight.

I looked on, contrasting the view with what I had just left behind me. I could see children just learning to walk, tottering around sometimes with and sometimes without the support of a parent, chuckling in delight and yelping in pleasure as they tumbled onto the grass and then found their feet again. How different, I thought to myself, from the children less than a mile away, many older than those I was now watching, but still unable to walk and still confined, and in some cases tied, within their cots in those foul-smelling rooms.

I should have been able to rest in that park and take pleasure in the surroundings of family life and normality. I could not. I felt an urge to approach those parents and demand how they could ignore the plight of those abandoned children in the nearby orphanage. Relaxation was beyond me and so, with a mixture of emotions, sadness, even bitterness and frustration, I trudged back to the hotel where I stood under the dribble from the shower, trying to wash away the taste of pollution and the smell of excreta. I toppled onto my bed, eventually, and tried to get some sleep.

***

In the early evening, I returned to reception, where I found Mircea. Had he had any luck in contacting his interpreter friend?

"No," he said. "I'm very sorry but I think he must have been away for the weekend and he has not replied to my messages. I'll keep trying and maybe I will have some better news for you tomorrow."

I turned away disappointed before I remembered that I had arranged for Carmel to ring me that evening.

"Mircea," I said. "My wife has promised to ring me this evening, and I would be very grateful if you would ensure that I can receive a call when it comes in."

"Sure," he said, "there should be no problem. It's better that you try and take the call at the front desk, since I wouldn't like to have the call cut off because of a bad connection to your room."

I couldn't quite understand why it was that the call might get lost, but I didn't have a problem receiving the call anywhere, just as long as I could hear her voice.

"It'll come in at around 7pm Romanian time," I said, "and I'll make sure that I'm close by."

With that, I wandered back to the dining room and settled down for another modest meal. The waitress appeared once more and I felt that it would be kind if I gave her a pack of Kent. She brightened up immediately, and I asked if there was any possibility that I might have a bottle of wine. I knew the Romanian word was *vin*, just like the French, but I had absolutely no idea how to pronounce it, so I accompanied the word by pointing at the glass on my table and making drinking gestures.

It seemed to work, because shortly she brought out a tall thin bottle, reminiscent of a German 'hock' bottle. It was already open, with what looked like a pretty battered cork protruding halfway from the spout. For all I knew, it has simply been refilled, although with what I was not entirely sure. I poured a glass of yellowish liquid and held it up to the light. It was, at least, clear, although horribly sweet tasting. I thanked her as graciously as I could, and sat back once more, trying to make head or tail of the Watchmaker.

After about a quarter of an hour, a husband and wife and a young boy of about seven came into the room with an older woman and sat down at a table behind me. Since there was no one else in the room, and since there was otherwise complete silence, I could not help but overhear their conversation. It was immediately apparent that the couple and the boy were Danish. The older woman, clearly, was an interpreter, provided, presumably, by the government tourist agency. I gleaned all this immediately because their conversation was carried out in English. Clearly, Danish was not a language high up on the menu of common languages in Romania, but equally plainly, given that Danes invariably have a good grasp of English, they had taken the sensible choice of securing an English-speaking interpreter for their visit.

I wondered, initially, what on earth they were doing in this rather second-rate hotel when, I assumed, the three of them were on holiday. It then became plain. They were on their way to the Black Sea, to, presumably, a popular coastal resort, and had had to break their journey in Bucharest, given that there were no direct flights from Denmark.

I listened, fascinated by their conversation with the interpreter. They clearly expected that there might be some rather better food and drink available during their stopover but they were to be sadly disappointed.

"Can I order a Coke for my son?" I heard the father ask.

I could sense the embarrassment in the interpreter's voice when she explained that that was not possible in this hotel.

I sensed an opportunity and decided not to be embarrassed. I waited a few moments and then got up from the table and took the bottle of wine across to the family.

"I hope you don't mind me intruding," I said, "but I couldn't fail to overhear that you would rather like a drink of something rather more substantial than just water."

I carried on before they could interrupt me or protest. "Please," I said, "with my compliments have the rest of this wine which I ordered tonight. I have no more use for it and you might enjoy it."

"That's very kind of you," said the father.

"It's nothing at all," I said, "but I wonder if in return I might ask you a favour?"

He looked at me quizzically.

"You have an interpreter with you," I said. "As it happens, I need an interpreter. At the moment, I'm struggling to find one, and I would be most grateful if I could have a word with this lady shortly before she leaves this evening."

"But of course you may," he said. The interpreter herself nodded and said that she would see me later if I might wait in the reception area.

I left the dining room and sat in the reception area, patiently waiting for the interpreter to emerge, which she did about forty-five minutes later. I went across to her and immediately noticed that in her lapel was a Christian 'fish' brooch.

I introduced myself and told her straight away that I recognised the pin in her jacket. She looked down at it and then back at me.

"You see," I said, "I am a member of the congregation of a cathedral in England. In fact, I sing in the choir and have done for some years."

She relaxed. "That's wonderful," she said, "and how nice to meet a fellow Christian." This was a sentiment which I shared, notwithstanding my modest embarrassment at being identified by my faith. She told me her name was Beatrice and that she worked part-time for the government tourist office.

"Look," I said. "I realise that this is rather impertinent, but I need the help of a translator, an interpreter, to help me with my endeavour to adopt a child from one of the orphanages in Bucharest. I have an appointment, on Monday, to meet a social worker and quite possibly the mother of the child, and without an interpreter, I think I'm going to have problems."

"To be honest," she said, "I don't know much about these orphanages but I will be very happy to help you, and if you can give me the address and the time, I'll meet you there, and…" as if to forestall my next suggestion "…you must not think of asking me to accept any money."

I was so grateful, I didn't know what to say. So I thanked her and, giving her the address, I promised to meet her on Monday.

I sat down to wait for the promised phone call and, sure enough, moments after seven o'clock, Mircea beckoned me over. "There's a phone call for you and I suppose it must be your wife since it has come from England. You can take it on that phone down at the end of the desk, where you should not be disturbed."

He pointed to the end of the counter, where there was some sort of open phone booth, and I went across and picked up the telephone. The line was pretty crackly but I was able to hear Carmel's voice.

"I had to put my mother on a plane this morning," I said, "so I'm here alone. I've found a child but I'm very worried about him. I can't seem to get any response out of him, and for all I know, he might be deaf, let alone what else might be wrong with him. I expected some eye contact, at least, but nothing I could do seemed to register. I can't tell you how ghastly this all is and how insecure I feel. What if the poor thing is brain damaged or so developmentally delayed that we end up with a hospital case?"

I realised that I was babbling and not making much sense. Yet at the same time, I was horribly confused and still shocked by what I had seen in both the orphanages. Carmel was the only person I could share this with, and yet here I was, not making a great deal of sense on the phone, unloading my insecurity without any compensating suggestions, let alone sensible alternatives.

"Any sort of paediatric overview is simply unobtainable. I really am stuck and don't know what to do for the best."

Carmel did her best to sound sympathetic. "Just make sure you bring him home," she said. "Failure is not an option."

Wow. She knew just how to rally the troops! I realised, of course, that this was not a time to feel sorry for myself and that I was imagining things if I thought that this would ever be an easy ride. Of course I had to get him out of that place and, as Carmel said, failure was not an option.

I told her I loved her, and reluctantly rang off, marginally encouraged. I decided that I would go back to Hotel Lido and make contact with the nurses, thinking that it might be a good idea to perhaps swap one of my supplies for one of the many toys poking out of sacks that I had seen in their room, in the hope that I might generate a spark of something in the little boy. So, with a bottle of Hibiscrub in my rucksack, I set off for the city once more.

***

Walking rather more briskly this time, I was at Hotel Lido shortly before eight o'clock, where I made my way to the nurses' room. Liz and Anna were there, and seemed pleased to see me.

"I'm sorry," I said, "but I need to share this with you. I'm very worried about the little boy I've found. He shows no response, and is so out of it that he could be deaf. He can't walk properly and he seems to find it difficult even to hold up his head. There's no eye contact, and…" I tailed off, miserably.

"I understand completely," said Liz, "but trust me, these children are like little flowers who've never been given the chance to open. As soon as you show this little chap the love and affection that he's never had, the transformation will be miraculous. You need to believe that. I came across a woman a few days ago who actually changed her mind at the airport and left this poor little girl behind, saying that she didn't believe that the child would ever improve. That was a dreadful thing to do and so unjustified. The child was just waiting for love and care and would have responded so well. Don't let that happen to this little boy, whatever you do."

I remained silent, trying to digest what she was saying.

"Okay," I said, finally. "But I just had to share this with somebody. I need somehow to keep a grip on reality, and at the moment I'm in something of a daze."

I said that I was planning to go back to the orphanage the next day to try some sort of bonding exercise. I needed to see whether he would respond, however modestly, to a display of affection aimed solely at him, and I wanted to see whether, somehow, I could start helping him.

I asked whether she could let me have one of the toys from the sacks scattered around the room.

"Of course," she said. "Here, let me help you choose."

Immediately she came up with a plastic toy consisting of five rings, all increasing in size, like multicoloured doughnuts, all of which fitted on to a small rod, itself embedded into a plastic base.

"Try that. It might show that he has some manual co-ordination and perhaps that he understands what to do with the rings, and in what order."

I tried to tell her how kind she was, but ended up simply swapping the toy for the Hibiscrub, before I wished them goodnight and said that I hoped to see them again.

Back, then, to the hotel and bed. Mircea was no longer on duty so I went straight to my room and put my head down to sleep – not an easy task, given my experiences that day. But I managed to sleep, and woke vaguely refreshed the next morning.

After managing a couple of cups of black tea and some stale bread, I went straight to the orphanage. It was Sunday, and Ursuliano was not there; I decided to go straight in.

I came across the orderly to whom I had given my small offerings the previous day, and she beckoned me to the backyard and told me to wait. A few minutes later, my foundling was brought into the yard, wearing a tiny T-shirt and a pair of small blue nylon shorts, although without shoes or socks. He appeared comparatively clean, and tottered uncertainly towards me.

There were no other children around, and the orderly smiled at me and retreated back to the door, leaving me to my own devices.

I looked at little Petre George. I knew that in that part of the world, names were, to English ears, back to front. So, this was George.

He did not return my stare. Having picked him up, I had put him gently down and I sat on the ground watching him as he wandered around me. He clearly found it difficult to walk, but for the most part, he remained upright, pausing every now and again to examine a brightly coloured insect which was scampering through the dust at his feet.

I spoke to him softly, but there was no response.

Gradually, although his face had clearly been cleaned up, green mucus started to appear from his nose. Then, to his apparent surprise, he began to urinate, allowing the warm liquid to trickle down his leg onto the ground to form a puddle where he stood.

He appeared only vaguely interested in his wider surroundings and seemed to pay no attention to me at all, even when I held out my hand and tried to hold one of his.

I decided that I would take out the toy and see whether that might generate any interest at all. Holding the rod at its base in one hand, I showed him one of the coloured rings and very slowly and deliberately placed it on to the rod and let it slide down to the base. I repeated that with every ring and watched his face as I did so.

Did I detect a flicker of interest? I tried not to imagine it but repeated the exercise several times. I made sure that I placed the rings in order, the fattest one on the bottom, and the thinnest, smaller ring, on the very top, forming a cone of rings on the pole.

Eventually, taking one of the rings off but leaving all the others on the pole, I handed it to him.

"Come on, old chap," I said softly. "Show me what you're made of."

He took the ring, and let it drop onto the ground.

I picked it up and very slowly and deliberately put it back on the pole. Trying to ensure that he did not look away, I repeated the exercise. He, too, repeated his response, dropping the ring on the ground.

I did it again – and so did he. So I changed tactics. This next time, I emptied the pole of all the rings and simply held one of them in my right hand and placed it slowly and carefully onto the pole, held in my left.

He looked intently at what I had done. I pushed my left hand towards him, holding the base of the pole, and pushed the one ring to the very top before letting it fall back to the base.

For the first time, he reached towards the ring, and pulled it off himself.

"Now," I said, "let's see you put it back on again."

He looked at the ring in his hand, and very slowly pushed it against the tip of the pole, twisting and turning it until it slid back on, and on down to the base. I could have hugged him, but sensing that he was still unready for tactile contact of that nature, I gently cupped his face in my two hands.

"You are a beautiful, clever boy." I tried to look at his eyes but he looked at the ground and at the dust on his feet. I felt a tear form at the corner of one of my eyes.

I sat back and gave him another ring. Emboldened by his success, he immediately put it on the pole, then another, until all of them were on the pole in varying positions. So I took them all off and gave him the biggest one which he again put on the pole until it slid down to the base. Then I gave him the next size and so on until he had built the perfect cone. Now for the big test. I took them all off and laid them on the ground, in order, to see whether he might follow the logic of that order and put them on sequentially.

This, of course, was too much. He put them all back on, but not in order. I told myself not to be too ambitious, but to take comfort in what was already an amazing step forward.

We played together, like this, for about an hour. He would wander off from time to time, barely keeping his balance, and then totter back, to pick up either a ring or the pole which he would then put together and pull apart. It didn't take him long to discover that it was possible to make the ring roll on its side, but unfortunately, given the uneven and dusty state of the yard, all his attempts to have a ring roll for more than a few inches would come to grief.

Eventually, the same orderly appeared. What, I wondered, were her qualifications? Was she an orderly or a nurse for just some sort of assistant? She was wearing something approximating a uniform, but I doubted that she had any clinical qualifications. However, whether because of my small gifts, she appeared to be offering some kindness to us both, presumably as powerless in the face of these conditions as I was.

She lifted up the little boy, smiled at me, and said it was time that all the children were being fed. I decided to leave her to it, since I simply could not bear the sight of feeding time.

But it made one thing terribly clear in my mind. I had to get him out of there, and soon.

EIGHTEEN

"The world wants to be deceived."

Sebastian Brant, *Ship of Fools*, 1494

Having to wait out the balance of Sunday was an ordeal. There was nowhere to go other than the hotel, since I could not bear the sight of happy families in the park. I wandered into the city centre and found a state tourist office, which I assumed might give me some ideas as to what I might see in Bucharest, but it appeared that sightseeing was out of the question – the city had clearly only recently shaken off the ordeal of revolution, and the one clerk at the run-down desk in the office was unable to offer any suggestions as to what might be seen or how.

She offered me a set of postcards displaying various monuments from better days and asked me whether I had any loose change of money from England, since she was collecting coins from all over the world.

To her delight, I was able to hand over a few coins which I found in my pocket while she apologised for the state of the city in general and her office in particular. There were no brochures, maps, or even posters on display which might tempt the visitor to a day trip around Bucharest or the neighbouring countryside. The outlook was as gloomy as the windows of her office were dirty, so I trudged back to the hotel, deep in thought as to what the coming week would hold for me.

So, I mused to myself, I had found a child who was not, as I first feared, obviously disabled, although he was very clearly dreadfully behind in his development. But I felt an immediate attachment to him. I would get him out of that place and nothing, I felt, would stop me.

Had I known of the obstacles ahead, I might not have been so confident.

For the time being, however, my confidence levels had risen slightly, and when I returned to the reception desk in the hotel, I was not unduly anxious when I heard Mircea's news.

"I am really sorry," he said, in his precise way. "My friend at the embassy finally replied. He can't really help you, because he's too busy."

"Well, don't worry," I said. "By chance, I have found an interpreter who has promised to meet me tomorrow and I'm keeping my fingers crossed that she will come up trumps."

We spent the next few minutes defining what I meant by fingers and trumps, to his great delight.

"This will be really good for me when I go to England," he said. "Maybe you will come and see me at the hotel?"

"But look," he continued. "I have another friend, who I know has just left university, and he should now be on vacation. His name is Bogdan Simionescu, and he lives in Bucharest with his parents. Here is his telephone number – give him a call and see whether he is free."

On the now well tested and tried principle of one step forward and two steps back, I decided that it might be a very good idea to have a first reserve, so I asked Mircea to make the call and put me through. Once more back in the cubicle, I picked up the phone and was put through to a voice with a marked American accent.

Bogdan spoke perfect English. I explained that his name had been given to me by Mircea, and that it had been suggested that he might be able to act as interpreter for me.

"Sure," said Bogdan. "Absolutely no problem. I'm on vacation now and I have nothing planned."

"But," I replied, "I've already arranged an interpreter for a meeting tomorrow and, as far as I know, she is going to make herself available and will help me."

"OK."

"But having said that, I have never met this woman before, and neither of us know what is up ahead and it may be that she will only be available for this one meeting."

"Look," he replied, "Mircea has given you my number. I've got nothing planned for the next couple of weeks. If you need my help, just give me a call."

It was so strange, meeting these extremes of hostility and generosity in this bewildering country. Still, this was not the time to question my good fortune. I thanked him profusely and rang off.

Back in my room, after another unappetising meal of tomatoes and ham to which the waitress had been good enough to add a few chips, I tried to sleep. Downstairs, there seemed to be something of a party going on, but there wasn't quite the din that I had overheard at Hotel Lido, perhaps because the merrymakers were not quite so well-heeled. I turned on the television set in an attempt to pass the time. The black-and-white screen flickered, offering me a picture in two segments – at the top, about three inches of screen revealed the bottom portion of the picture, and the remaining ten inches or so of the screen portrayed what was in fact the top part and bulk of the picture.

The plot was impossible to follow, save that there were a number of camels, a lot of sand, and some murderous-looking tribesmen – the poor sound track was in French, and the Romanian subtitles were, given the faulty screen, superimposed at the top rather than the bottom of the picture. I had caught the last part of the feature, and as the credits rolled, the distinctive voice of Barbara Dixon pealed out, singing 'Caravan'. In English. I couldn't have made it up if I had tried.

Given that the programme which followed appeared to be some sort of news feature in Romanian, and that, on this crazy screen, the newsreader's forehead appeared under his chin, I searched for any other channel which might be broadcasting.

If it was, any thought of reception was beyond the capacity of this particular set, so I switched off and tried to get some sleep.

***

Next morning, I was awake early. At 6am I was up, fretting, unable to relax. I picked at my statutory bread roll, and sipped the tea, alone still in the surreal dining room.

I guessed that the social worker would probably put in an appearance at about 10am, and it would be a waste of time getting to the orphanage before 9am. I had arranged to meet Beatrice at 9.30am, so I made my way there, on foot, partly to pass the time, and partly to clear my head.

NINETEEN

"Behaviour of such cunning cruelty that only a
human being could have thought or contrived we call
'inhuman', revealing thus some pathetic ideal standard
for our species that survives all betrayals."

Rose Macaulay, *A Casual Commentary*, 1925

Monday morning at 9am. Feeling, for reasons quite beyond me, like an errant schoolboy, I arrived at the orphanage. I was not completely alone, for there were a number of people, mainly men in suits, wandering in and out of the gates. Standing there, watching them come and go, it gradually dawned on me that these might well be the lawyers I had heard of.

At 9.30am, true to her word, Beatrice, my faithful interpreter, arrived. She seemed slightly surprised at the run-down appearance of the building in front of which we were standing. It was pretty clear that she, like, I assumed, many others, had no idea what was behind the crumbling walls.

We greeted each other. "How kind of you to come and give up your time."

"No," she said, "I promised you that I would be here, and I want to support you as much as I can in your expedition."

We stood inside the rusting railings, set into and along the crumbling concrete which formed the front wall, extending along the pavement and fronting an area which would once, I suppose, have been landscaped. Standing where we were, looking outwards from the main complex, the gatehouse from which I had seen the fierce-looking *babushka* emerge when I first came to Orphanage Number One was now on our left. On our right, opposite *babushka haus* was its twin, a similar building, where I had met the social worker. It was there, I assumed that I would be meeting her today and I pointed it out to Beatrice.

There was not much more we could say to each other while we waited, standing uncomfortably on the potholed ground, there being no seats or bench to sit on. I was on tenterhooks, and Beatrice was clearly ill at ease, not knowing really what all this was about. Small talk was too difficult and I felt faintly guilty for bringing her into these surroundings. I, to a certain extent by then, had been ready for the scene which was clearly making Beatrice so uncomfortable now. I had seen the bricks, the scaffolding, the broken pieces of timber and the weeds. Worse, I had been inside and I'd seen the neglected and broken interior, and at least she had been spared that.

Ten o'clock came and went. There was much activity in the social work office, but no sign of the social worker. The men in suits appeared to be coming and going from the gatehouse, forming an incongruous moving tableau of smart and well-dressed people picking their way through the ruined forecourt. As I watched them, my impatience rose with every newcomer – impatience which soon translated into unease.

Eleven o'clock passed, and then noon, when suddenly, in a surreal entourage, the social worker swept in by the gate nearest to her office, pursued by a gaggle of more men in suits.

"That's the social worker who promised me that she would be here with the child's mother," I said to Beatrice. "She's dreadfully late and I suppose very busy, but I hope, when she finishes talking to all those people, that I will be able to introduce you to her."

How foolish I was. The social worker came to the door and appeared ready to move off once more. I ushered Beatrice over to her. I was anxious not to lose what appeared to be a dwindling opportunity to continue my dialogue, such as it was, with the social worker.

The social worker, once more heavily made-up and incongruous in her expensive-looking day clothes, which clashed with this background of squalor, spoke briefly to Beatrice. From her body language, I could tell that she was not keen to co-operate. The characteristic shrug of the shoulders, the dip of the head, the half turn away – the now familiar but immediately recognisable Romanian shrug. The discussion came to an abrupt halt.

Beatrice turned back to me, as the social worker pushed past her and left through the gate.

"I really don't know what's going on," she said. "But the social worker tells me that she might be able to bring the mother here after tomorrow."

"What on earth did she mean by that?" I asked. "What does she mean by 'after tomorrow'?" Did it mean the next day, the day after that, or sometime vaguely in the future?

"Well," Beatrice said, "it could be the next day, but one can never be sure. It's a common enough term in Romanian but does not specify a particular moment in time."

I looked gloomily around me. One step forward and two steps back appeared again to be my lot. I realised that I had been foolish to have relied upon the word of the social worker whom I very obviously could not trust.

Worse, I was becoming more convinced that the men in suits were, as I had suspected, lawyers or fixers, retained by agencies or even hopeful adopters, seeking to buy children with the assistance of the social worker and on the basis, presumably, of kickbacks from which she would profit. I reflected that, of course, she would have taken an immediate dislike to me because first, I was myself a lawyer, and secondly, I had no intention of paying money for a child, mainly from a sense of right and wrong but also because, of course, under English law it was illegal.

At that moment, Zoitsanu appeared, shuffling across the debris in the front of the orphanage. I waved to her and she appeared to recognise me and came over to us.

I introduced Beatrice to her, and Beatrice, bless her, for her part immediately addressed her in Romanian, relieving me of the task of speaking to them both in my distinctly average French.

After a moment, Beatrice turned to me. "She says that the social worker will be back this afternoon, but she is unsure when. She also said that the mother would be contacted sometime 'after tomorrow'."

I thought I ought to make my feelings clear. I expected, I said, to be treated with at least some courtesy, and despite recognising the difficulties under which they laboured, if I was given an appointment, which I had been, I expected it to be kept or at least, if it could not be, to be given a clear idea of the next step.

She turned back to Zoitsanu and must have said something along those lines, for Zoitsanu suddenly became quite animated. Gradually, her voice increased in volume. She spoke faster and faster and became red in the face. In the torrent of words , I picked out the word 'negre'. And as she said it she almost spat on the ground.

Poor Beatrice physically recoiled from this confrontation and was clearly very distressed by it. Zoitsanu turned on her heel and shuffled away from us while Beatrice drew breath. She turned back to me, almost in tears.

"This is dreadful," she said. "That woman clearly does not like the child whom you have found. She has used words which I do not want to repeat to you. And I'm afraid that I can help you no longer. This is all far too distressing for me."

What could I say? Beatrice had been kind enough to agree to come to the orphanage, and she had done so not only promptly but without charge. She was an essentially good woman who had wanted to help me and I had no right to demand that she stay and continue with the task.

I forced myself to remain calm. "Beatrice, I quite understand and I'm very grateful for your help to this moment. Don't for one minute feel guilty. I am sure that I will find more help from other quarters. This is an unpleasant place and unpleasant things have happened here. I remain in your debt."

We shook hands and Beatrice walked away, with her shoulders slumped, clearly very unhappy. She did not look back.

***

What on earth was I to do now? I had thought that I had been dealt a better hand than this, but my cards were falling, one by one, to the floor. And now, this. No interpreter, and no co-operation from this social worker person. I walked through the gates and turned down the side of the orphanage, walking slowly along the pavement, head down, racking my brains as to what I could do.

This side street could have been in any suburb in any city of the world. More dusty, perhaps, but with substantial buildings set back behind high walls, trees spaced along the pavement on each side of the road, itself mercifully free of any motor traffic. There was nothing to suggest that on my right, behind yet another high wall, behind the railings and faceless bricks and peeling mortar, there were hundreds of deprived children living in utter squalor

I walked on and saw a telephone box. I remembered that I had had the sense to write down Bogdan's telephone number and that it was still in my pocket. But it was now after one o'clock in the afternoon. Would Bogdan be at home? Even if he was, would he be prepared to help me? I pulled open the door and tried to translate the instructions on the box below the handset. Thankfully, they were accompanied by pictures. I needed coins, and I was able, just, to work out the sequence of where to put the particular required denominations. And by a miracle, the few coins in my pocket, which to my mind had been virtually valueless, were enough, it seemed, to place a local call. If there was an area code, I did not know it and so more in hope than expectation, I inserted 20 lei, dialled the number on my slip of paper and waited.

And to my great relief, Bogdan picked up after just a couple of rings.

"Hello, Bogdan, it's Tony again."

"Hey, Tony, how are you?" His cheerful reply lifted my spirits immediately

"I've got problems," I said. "The interpreter whom I told you about on the phone this morning has jumped ship and I'm here on my own. I desperately need assistance."

"Then I'm your man. Tell me exactly where you are and I will come and meet you. I can use my father's car."

I gave him the name of the street on which I was standing, as phonetically precise as I could, and told him where the telephone box was.

"I'll be there in about 10 minutes," he said, "so hang on and we'll sort this out."

He rang off and I looked at the phone in my hand. Had the pendulum really swung back once more? Was I going to get help after all? There was absolutely no doubt in my mind now. Without an interpreter, and in the face of hostility, simply speaking to officials or professionals in my pretty basic French was not going to help me carry the day, and if Bogdan couldn't step up, then I really would be in trouble.

I found some shade and stood by the telephone box, trying not to think too hard about the options, waiting for Bogdan and perspiring heavily in the heat. Ten minutes passed and a light-blue Dacia pulled down the road and stopped opposite me. The driver got out and came across to me with a broad smile. Bogdan shook my hand vigorously and introduced himself in perfect English.

"Let's go and have a coffee and a juice," he said, setting off at a brisk walk, pausing only to remove the windscreen wipers on the car and lock them in the boot. He smiled apologetically. "They get taken, you know, and it is important that you keep hold of them!"

We headed for a small café where we sat at the central counter, and he ordered the drinks. The 'coffee' turned out to be rather weak Nescafe, and the 'juice' even weaker orange squash. But we were both thirsty, given the heat of the day and we dawdled over drinks, just like a good number of other young people, scattered around the tables in the café sitting and talking and smoking and passing the time of day. In stark contrast to what I had just left behind, the scene was utterly normal.

Bogdan told me that he had graduated that year from Bucharest University in dentistry, needing only an apprenticeship to become fully qualified. He lived with his mother and father closer to the centre of the city and had no brothers or sisters. He had no idea what employment prospects might exist, bearing in mind the recent revolution and the economic difficulties in the country.

"How come you speak English so perfectly," I asked.

"Well," he said, in an Americanised drawl, "it is taught in schools and, of course, I watch videos."

Another, quite startling, revelation. On the one hand, a country in turmoil, secret police around every corner, neighbour spying upon neighbour, shortages of food, staples, and essentials, visas to leave the country virtually unobtainable, quite extreme poverty and squalor visible at every glance – and yet from within the gloom, flashes of hope, exemplified by the extraordinary intelligence of this young man whose English was quite faultless, learned from a curriculum no better or worse than that available to English schoolchildren learning any European language, and from a meagre ration of American B movies.

The only downside, and one which we both found hilarious, was that his English was delivered with an incongruous American accent, and peppered with such Americanisms as 'you don't say'!

"And tell me, Tony, where do you come from?"

"I come, initially, from New Zealand, but for many years now I've lived in England. My wife and I now live near Coventry."

"Ah," said Bogdan, nodding sagely. "Moonlight Sonata."

"What do you mean?"

"You know," he said, looking surprised that I needed an explanation. "When Coventry was bombed, Goering called the raid 'Moonlight Sonata'. And we all know that Churchill knew that the raid was coming and that he took the decision not to move to reinforce the defences that were there, since otherwise the Germans would realise that he had found out in advance and his advantage of surprise, later in the war, would be lost."

I listened, astonished. How come a young Romanian student knew all this, when it did not even appear in most, or possibly in any, history books available to English schoolchildren of his generation? My respect for Romanian education, and for Bogdan's intelligence, increased the more we spoke.

And we spoke for more than an hour, getting to know each other, sharing jokes, and telling each other of our recent experiences. Bogdan, I learned, had been in the very first wave of protesters and had been present in what he called Revolution Square when the crowds and the protests finally persuaded the powers that be that the game was up.

He knew that corruption existed. Who didn't? And he knew that many children were accommodated in state care.

"Ceaușescu made contraception and abortion illegal, you know. Much of our industrial base has not really recovered from the war, and where he had no industrial base, he decided that workers could take the place of machines. He encouraged childbirth, and if families couldn't cope, he encouraged them to hand the children over to the state."

This was what Graham Prestridge had told me, and it had been repeated by Dominic, the volunteer nurse.

But Bogdan didn't know the dreadful conditions of the orphanages which had been identified by Western journalists, and he listened quietly and soberly to my own halting description of what I had encountered and what I had yet to do.

I told him about the social worker. "She is a strange kettle of fish," I said.

"A what?"

"Kettle of fish … it's a saying the Brits have when they want to describe a mixed character – usually in less than complimentary terms."

"You don't say," exclaimed Bogdan.

"No, Bogdan, you don't say 'you don't say'."

We roared with laughter.

"And what about this Zulu person?"

"No," I said, "Zoitsanu."

"Ah, Zoitsanu. What's her problem?"

I explained how she had spoken to Beatrice and that I had heard 'negre'.

"Hmm," said Bogdan. "You see, Romanians are racist people."

"What do you mean?"

"Have you seen any black people around?"

"Well, no," I said, "but that doesn't make the population racist."

"You might think so, but you'd be surprised. The child was described as 'negre' because, in Zoitsanu's view, he is not white. Probably if he were Hungarian, Albanian, or God help us, Russian, he would be hated just as much."

I was lost for words and had nothing useful to contribute. But I had to agree that it was time to do something.

"Okay," he said. "We don't have a minute to lose. We shall go back to the orphanage and we'll find out just what is going on."

And so, into the mid afternoon, we both walked back to the orphanage and, at Bogdan's suggestion, straight into the social worker's office. Where we found the lady herself, at that moment free from the attention of any hovering lawyer.

She flashed me a look of barely concealed hostility as Bogdan immediately warmed to his task. He was not deflected by her sour expression, and as she tried to avoid discussion, he followed her around the room, without raising his voice, maintaining a calm delivery with a pleasant smile. If she wanted to provoke him, she was mistaken and the more it was clear that he would not be deflected by her unpleasantness, the more unsettled she seemed to become.

Eventually, as if to try and shake him off, she went to a drawer and extracted a file and produced a small piece of paper which she thrust at him, reading out extracts from the file as she did so. Then, satisfied that she had done and said enough, she closed the file, put it back in the drawer, and glared at us both.

I ignored her and listened to Bogdan.

"This woman says that she knows where the child's mother is working. She has given me the address and she says that if I make contact with her, she will co-operate in releasing the child for adoption. She will herself contact the mother to tell her that we are on our way. So, I suggest we leave now."

And that was it?

Bogdan ushered me away, out of the office and through the gate. Only when we had turned the corner and had returned to his father's car did he exhale with a sigh of relief.

"Tony," he said, "that is one unpleasant woman, but we will get the better of her, I promise. And here's a start." He dug in his pocket and pulled out the piece of paper that the social worker had showed him and forgotten to take back from him when she shut the file.

It was George's birth certificate.

TWENTY

"A true friend is the most precious of all possessions and
the one we take least thought about acquiring."

La Rochefoucauld, *Maxims*, 1665

Without breaking stride, Bogdan got in the car,
talking as he did so.

"The government requires all citizens to
carry identification with them at all times – so we all have
identity cards. Without the card, we can do nothing, go
nowhere. And children don't have cards, so they rely on
their birth certificates. And we now have this kid's identity.
Without it, the orphanage and that horrible woman can't
move him around, so at least we know that he is staying put."

I was lost in admiration for his quick thinking. But
what about the mother?

"She works at a tractor factory in Stanesti, about a
hundred miles from here, and that's where we're going now."

I was both astonished and humbled by his unconditional
acceptance of the challenge which, in his view, now faced
us both.

"We will be brothers in this," he smiled mischievously.
"We have a saying in Romania. 'Come in through the door.

If you can't get in that way, then try the window'."

Well, however ungainly the image, I understood what he meant. I had an ally – and what an ally he would turn out to be.

While Bogdan drove through the outskirts of Bucharest, I examined the birth certificate. There was the birthday – 11 May 1988. So, little Petre George was not 'almost two' at all. He was approaching two and a half. Time was marching on.

We followed the dusty main road out of Bucharest, squeezing past filthy lorries belching smoke, which Bogdan told me were probably on their way to and from Bulgaria, although carrying what was anyone's guess. There was an occasional, usually empty, flat-bed farm wagon, on car tyres, pulled by an emaciated-looking horse, driven on by depressed-looking individuals sometimes alone, sometimes in huddled family groups. From time to time, he had to brake hard, swerving around jagged ravines where the tarmac had long since disappeared. Through the utterly depressing countryside we passed overgrown fields without any sign of either crops or livestock.

"You know, when I flew in, the countryside was just like this. Nothing seemed to be growing and the whole area seemed to be devoid of life."

"It is a tragedy," said Bogdan. "The people don't have enough money to pay for food and the farmers don't have the money to invest in the production of food. It's a downward cycle. You know, Romania used to be such a productive country but since the Communists took over, because of the state of the country, they took the view that economies of scale would rescue the agricultural industry, and so vast co-operatives were set up. And the problem with co-operatives is that the Communists would set a quota, and the labourers would aim for that quota and nothing more. Once it was reached, they would perhaps take a little more for themselves or their families, but the remaining crops would simply be put to the torch or left to rot . The quotas were stupidly low, but no one complained."

We contemplated this depressing scenario for a moment.

"And do you know that before the war, the staple price of wheat for the whole of Europe was actually set in the bourse in Bucharest."

We shared a further silence until I broke the mood. "You don't say."

We both laughed.

"We have had more than our share of bad luck," he continued after some time. "The Germans wanted our oilfields at the outset of war, and we weren't in any position to resist, so we aligned ourselves with the Axis powers.

"Then, as Germany faced defeat and the Allies advanced from the west, the Russians took the opportunity to sweep us up with the rest of Eastern Europe, and we were thrown from the frying pan into the fire." Bogdan was clearly pleased with his use of English.

Yes, I thought. Wrong place at the wrong time. From what little I knew about geo-political ebbing and flowing, Romania had been in a position of enormous potential at the crossroads of the trade routes between Europe and Byzantium, a position which had terrible consequences when the Third Reich sought to dominate the continent.

As we drove, I noticed that if there were any other cars on the road, they only appeared to be of two types – the Dacia, the make that Bogdan was driving, and the Trabant, which I recognised as the 'little stinker', which had been the main, if not the only, means of private transport throughout East Germany, deriving its name from the smelly exhaust fumes produced by its two-stroke engine.

"That's right," said Bogdan. "We have no car industry of our own to speak of. You've probably noticed that the car is in fact the old French Renault. Private citizens get to drive either white or light-blue Dacias. The secret police get to drive black ones. Good camouflage, eh?" He laughed. "But look at the state of it. It's a new car that has done very few miles but there are problems with it already. You can see that here and there the interior is starting to fall to bits."

He was right. The cheap plastic mouldings which had been inexpertly applied to the doors and the fascia now appeared to be about to fall off. The minimal upholstery was stark and uncomfortable. The bodywork had certainly lost whatever showroom shine it might have had when it was bought. I recognised the salty taste in my mouth and knew that it contained sulphur, and that the rain would dilute and combine with the polluted air to form a mild but deadly acid which would simply eat away at the body surface, leaving a dull and almost sandpapery feel to it.

Still, by good fortune, I had obviously secured the help of a willing interpreter and guide, if not friend, and we were mobile.

***

We motored on through the afternoon until we reached Stanesti, an unremarkable town which seemed, like so many areas of Romania that I had seen so far, to have closed in on itself. Bogdan found a lone pedestrian, who pointed out where the factory was.

We parked outside the factory gates. It appeared wholly lifeless. There was a gatehouse, but the red-and-white pole which would normally require traffic entering or leaving to stop and identify itself was, it seemed, permanently in the vertical, and I couldn't see any gatekeeper. If there was any activity at all, it was well away from the road, and whereas I had assumed that we might hear some signs of industry, there was utter silence.

"Don't worry," said Bogdan. "I know what to do and I will find out who to ask." And off he went. I sat in the car. It was stiflingly hot, so I wound down the windows and attempted to sleep.

The minutes stretched into an hour. Finally, Bogdan returned and got into the car.

"We've been – how do you say – led a dance," he said. "She's not there, and she hasn't been there for two years." Then quickly, no doubt seeing the look of despair on my face, he continued, "But don't worry, I got hold of some sort of personnel official, and he has given me her address. And believe it or not, if it is right, she is living in Bucharest."

Wonderful! We had been sent on a wild goose chase of rather more than 200 miles.

But Bogdan appeared not to be fazed at all. I insisted on giving him enough money so that he could fill up with petrol, and without any reduction in his cheerfulness we retraced our steps. The afternoon was wearing on and it was pointless our attempting to find her whereabouts that day and so Bogdan decided that he would take me back to Hotel Parc, and pick me up the next day. There was nothing much more we could do.

TWENTY ONE

"To say that man is made up of strength and weakness, of insight and blindness, of pettiness and grandeur, is not to draw up an indictment against him: it is to define him."

Diderot, *Addition aux Pensées philosophiques*, c.1762

Early next morning, I found Bogdan chatting to Mircea at reception. He greeted me like an old friend. "Let's go, Tony. We have someone to find!"

In fact, as we climbed into his father's car, neither of us had much idea where we might find her. Bogdan had the address which the factory official had given to him, but it was in a sector of Bucharest which he knew little about.

"Tell you what," I said. "I remember being completely lost in a town in England some years ago and, after driving in circles for a while, I decided to pay a taxi driver to lead me to the address."

"That sounds a great idea," said Bogdan. I had already shown him some of my 'provisions' as we were motoring to Stanesti. "Give me a packet of Kent, and when we find a taxi, we'll do just that."

We did, finally, find a taxi in the city centre, parked up against the kerb, and Bogdan got out and spent a few moments talking to the driver, showing him the address that we needed to find. I could see the driver through his back window, nodding his head and appearing to be comparatively enthusiastic, particularly when I saw Bogdan hand him the cigarettes.

Moments later, Bogdan returned to our car and our two vehicles set off in convoy.

"The taxi driver knows the area. He says it's well known for smuggling and other not entirely honest dealings. He's not too sure of the exact address but he said that he'll get us into what he called 'Kent Road'. That's where they smuggle the cigarettes, you know," he said, smiling.

Fifteen minutes later, the taxi pulled to the side and the driver beckoned Bogdan to his window once more. More discussions took place before the taxi drove away with a cheerful wave from the driver.

Bogdan came back to our car. "He thinks it's just a bit further down here, and gave me some rough directions. I reckon that when I get closer, there's bound to be someone I can ask."

We drove slowly into narrower streets, until Bogdan found a passer-by. There was a very brief conversation, and after a few words and some pointing down the street, the man scurried away.

"You know," said Bogdan, grinning, " I believe he thought I might be Securitate!"

"What, in a blue car?!" We laughed.

I looked him up and down. Sure enough, he was wearing

a particularly clean T-shirt, some foreign-looking jeans and a modern-looking pair of trainers. If he wasn't quite a mirror image of the men I saw in Bacau, there was still a flavour of individuality, and I supposed that anyone who was not particularly keen to have a brush with authority might, in this fragile climate, be suspicious of anybody who appeared self-possessed and in freshly laundered clothes.

"Anyway," he continued, "I've been given the exact address. I suggest we park up just round the corner, and I'll go and do some investigating. You'd better stay in the car. You look pretty out of place, here, and anyway, I don't want anyone taking the wheels off!"

I was happy enough with that, and a few moments later, Bogdan parked and left me in the car.

He was gone, in fact, for close on half an hour. When he returned, he said nothing, and kept his face impassive until we had driven a few blocks away. Then he parked up again and turned to me with a smile.

"I found her. She wasn't particularly happy to see me but when I showed her the birth certificate and told her what we were after, she made it clear that she would co-operate with us. She wasn't happy because she has at least three other children, possibly four. I think she is married and I think, too, that she doesn't want her family to know of the child which she had put in the orphanage. So she wants to be sure of my discretion and she has promised to do everything necessary to ensure that you can adopt him."

The pendulum had swung back. We had found the mother and she had, at least verbally, given her consent to the adoption. Now we had to embark on the formalities.

I explained to Bogdan that I had a checklist which, following the instructions of the Marriotts, I had set out as clearly as possible, showing stage by stage what I needed to do. First and foremost I needed the translated copy of my home study report and its accompanying documents, all of which I had handed over to Lily when I had first arrived in Bucharest.

Lily worked, I told him, in what she called the Notary's office, and by now she would have had my documents prepared.

"I know where that is," he said. "We'll go there now."

So, without hesitation, he drove us both back to the city centre and parked close to a large circular-looking office building which we entered through large imposing doors.

Inside, there was chaos. Or at least, that is how it seemed to me. There was the inevitable melee of people all clutching documents and all striving to get in front of each other. The din was quite extraordinary. Men were shouting, and women appeared to be screaming and, had I not known better, I would have imagined that there was some sort of medical crisis. The scene could have sprung from a picture by Hieronymus Bosch. Bogdan, however, seemed quite unmoved by our surroundings and was faintly amused when I protested that it was quite an extraordinary way to behave.

"Romanians are temperamental people," he said. "No one worries about shouting and screaming – it's all part of the act. All we need to do," he gestured towards one of the two doors at the rear of the room "is to quietly go through here and speak to the Notary."

And sure enough, without further ado, he led me around the scrum and eased us both through the door and into an oasis of quiet. He shut the door behind us, leaving the hubbub muted but not entirely cut off, and led me through an empty office and through another side door, into what appeared to be a secretaries' enclave.

There were two knee-hole desks in this small room, with an ancient typewriter on each. A dumpy middle-aged woman was behind one of them, with a small dog at her feet. Behind the other was Lily, who appeared to recognise me straight away and who smiled a greeting.

"I've got your papers here," she said, immediately. "I'm just finishing off this last page and you can take them with you."

Bogdan and I sat down on some chairs at the side of the room while I looked around. The facilities that these secretaries had to work with were pretty primitive. The paper they were using was desperately rough and thin. Neither of the women had any sort of India rubber or alteration fluid, and it appeared that if they did make a mistake, they had to scratch the letter or the word off the page with a razor blade. The typewriters appeared to be large, clumsy antiques which must have taken a considerable effort to operate. The exercise was obviously not one which could be completed at speed.

While we sat there, the dumpy woman decided that she would give us the benefit of her opinion of the children in the orphanages and the whole issue of adoption.

"You're wasting your time adopting a child from these places. They are full of gypsies who are thieves and vagabonds. They will never be any good and you will be taking a criminal into your house."

I sat silently for a moment, digesting her diatribe. Here was a different kind of unpleasantness which both distressed and angered me.

"Madam," I finally retorted across the room, "let us assume that your pessimistic commentary is accurate and that no sooner is a child brought out of one of these disgusting places in your country, but he begins to commit criminal acts. We have places for criminals in my country. They're called prisons. And I can assure you that the conditions in our prisons are a thousand times better than the conditions in your orphanages. I would be doing him a favour.

"Oh, and no doubt you treat this delightful-looking dog better, too, than the way in which your government is treating these children."

Her chubby face darkened with fury. I had spoken slowly enough to ensure that she would be able to digest every word that I had said and translate it in her nasty little mind.

Mercifully, Lily had finished her translation, and she hurriedly passed the papers to Bogdan, who sensed the beginning of a confrontation. He ushered me out of the office, back into the main office in which, now, some sort of official was sitting. He turned out to be the Notary Public, perhaps one of a number.

Bogdan and I went across and sat opposite him and proffered my paperwork, both the original, in English, and the translation, now handed over by Lily. Bogdan spoke rapidly to the Notary who glanced through the papers and then began stamping them.

It seems to be a curious feature of Eastern Europe that a great deal is made of rubber stamps. Any opportunity seems to be taken to stamp a document, the assumption being that the more stamps, seals or marks of an official-looking nature, the more valid or important the document must be.

Certainly, the Notary was well practised in the art of stamping, and he went about his task with gusto, the banging of the stamp on the pad and then the paperwork merging into the monotonous regularity of a Gatling gun. Within a short time, every page had a series of purple stamps of different sizes, and the Notary finally sat back, pleased with his handiwork. Bogdan handed over a number of hundred lei notes, we gathered up our documents and, leaving the office, pushed our way through the throng to the outside world. Once more, the tumult was deafening and disorganised.

"We call that 'Bedlam'," I said as we emerged into the street.

"You don't say. We call it normal!"

TWENTY TWO

"We humans are such limited creatures – how is it
that there are so few limits when it comes to human
suffering?"

Pierre Marivaux, *La Vie de Marianne*, 1731–41

At some stage we were going to have to obtain some
sort of history of our little boy and an up-to-date
medical report. For the report, the Department
of Health insisted upon the completion of a pro forma
provided by BAAF, the British Agencies for Adopting and
Fostering. The trouble was, I had no history and I had no
idea either who would complete the medical report.

"Let's go back to the orphanage," Bogdan suggested.
"Maybe the Director will give us some clue as to who we
ask and where we find things."

"OK," I said. "That seems a pretty good start."

So we drove back to the orphanage and, instead of
presenting ourselves either to the social worker or the
babushka, we went straight to the Director's office.

Today, neither of his two shapely secretaries seemed to be
around, so we knocked and went straight in to his drawing
room. Once again, he recognised me – who couldn't? I was

running out of T-shirts, and I looked no smarter than I had when I first met him.

Bogdan introduced himself in Romanian and the two spoke for a moment while I observed that that the young man whom I had seen on my previous visit was again with Ursuliano. The attention of both men was on Bogdan, so I looked a little more carefully at this other man. He, even more than Bogdan, had a look about him. I realised immediately what it was – it was sinister. However, he smiled at me when Bogdan had finished, and both he and Ursuliano professed that they were pleased to see us both. Uncertain whether or not the other man spoke French, I felt that it would be more polite to let Bogdan do all the talking in Romanian, since I knew that he would keep me fully up to speed either then or later.

He was asking Ursuliano a number of questions and it appeared that Ursuliano was struggling to find answers. Eventually, he took out a pad and wrote down an address and handed it to Bogdan, who folded it up, rose from his seat and wished both men a cheerful "Revedere."

He took me by the arm and ushered me out, wrinkling his nose at the smell as we went. When we had got out of the building, he said "You know, Tony, I don't think that Ursuliano is a medical doctor – or even a doctor of any sort."

"Funny, that," I said, "I don't either." And I told him about Ursuliano's behaviour with the skin medication.

"And that other chap," said Bogdan, "I'm a bit wary of him myself."

He fell silent for a moment, before continuing. "I can tell you that there have been stories that Ceaușescu would take the fitter inmates from these places and recruit them as Securitate."

"Seriously?"

I had heard that children would be bought by various means and Sadovici told me that children were actively sold to the French. But as Securitate?

"Think about it. You want blind obedience to the state, and you want to produce people who have no compunction about carrying out their orders, and no conscience or pity for the victims. What can be more ideal than taking a child who has no parents and no attachments and substituting the state?"

Was this paranoia or might it be true? Certainly, I had my doubts about the man whom I had now twice seen talking to Ursuliano and, of course, I and Bogdan both had our doubts about Ursuliano himself. Still, it wasn't our business. For the moment, anyway, Ursuliano appeared to be co-operative, and whatever the identity of the other man, he had not interfered. And of course, there wouldn't be any problem with attachment if Bogdan was right.

"What was the address he gave you?"

"Ah, yes," said Bogdan, getting back to our task. "There is a doctor who visits the orphanage, and she will complete a medical on George's current presentation. We can come back later this week when she'll be here. You can give me that form and I'll have Lily translate it, and when the doctor has completed it, we'll have it translated back again.

"But, as for historical medical records, they are not kept at the orphanage, and he has told me where we can find them. I don't imagine that there will be very much, but at least we can find out whether there is a record of his state of health when he was born. We can drive there now."

And off we went, Bogdan driving without complaint to a facility on the outskirts of the city. It had all the appearance of a large, purpose-built hospital, constructed, perhaps, in the late 19th century. And on the afternoon that we appeared, it was almost deserted. The main reception desk was manned by a bored-looking clerk, who gave Bogdan directions through a maze of corridors and stairwells, until we finally found ourselves at the end of one wing on the third floor. There was nobody about but, undeterred, Bogdan strode to the door at the end of the corridor and knocked.

After some moments, an irritable female voice answered from inside the door. Bogdan whispered to me that this was a doctor who Ursuliano said was in charge of administration of all the city orphanages and who, he now imagined, until that moment, might have been taking an afternoon nap. He knocked again. Silence. He looked at me. "Don't worry, I'm not giving up."

He knocked again, louder and longer.

This time, grumbling from behind the door, footsteps and finally, the handle rattled and the door flew open, revealing a dishevelled and very cross-looking woman in a white coat.

I didn't need to translate her immediate outburst. Her body language and her angry words were pretty plain. Bogdan looked at her calmly and spoke to her at some length, in Romanian.

The scowl never left her face, but when he had finished, she turned back into her office and beckoned him to follow.

I remained outside, listening to their conversation as she moved around the office and opened and shut a number of drawers.

It was perfectly plain that she continued to complain and grumble about being disturbed, while Bogdan managed to remain calm throughout. Eventually, when they both reappeared, I couldn't restrain myself any longer.

I went up to her, forcing a smile on my lips. She looked at me with something bordering on contempt.

"Madam, I anticipate that you call yourself a doctor. I have to congratulate you on your ability to show such compassion and care for the children who have been put in such wonderful surroundings. Angels and archangels must look on you with envy and admiration. Your attitude humbles me and I am privileged to have come into your presence."

There was a snort from behind her, as Bogdan tried, unsuccessfully, to hide his amusement. The woman turned to him and said something while he struggled to compose his features.

"She is asking whether or not you are actually being polite because she senses that you might not be," he said, doing his best to control himself.

"Tell her what you like. She can go to hell, where she belongs," I said over my shoulder, moving back down the corridor.

We left her, with her mouth hanging open, while Bogdan overtook me and led me out of the building. "Don't worry, we've got at least something."

He showed me a sheet of paper which, at first glance, didn't tell me very much. "What is it?"

"It's a record of the boy's APGAR scores when he was born." I had no idea what he was talking about, but he went on "That, at least, is something, and shows that it was a healthy birth. That nasty woman also told me that all the other records, such as they are, will be with the social worker, in her office... less, of course, the birth certificate!"

We got back in the car. "What now?"

"Well," I said, "I'm not entirely sure how this works, but had we not been in Bucharest, we would have been thinking of finding the local mayor."

Bogdan pondered this for a moment. "I think that it might be a good idea to go to the head office of the social services department, to see whether they have any suggestions." He threw the car into gear. "And for that, we go to the city hall."

***

Back, then, to the city hall, somewhere in the middle of Bucharest. We found ourselves driving along wide streets, following the course of the river Danube. Had the buildings and the streets been in better repair, this part of the city would have looked handsome, if not beautiful, but our attention was devoted to avoiding some enormous potholes which, had Bogdan not been keeping his eyes on the road, would have caused serious damage to the car's suspension and possibly even pulled off one or two wheels.

"Look over there," he said, pointing to an enormous building at the end of a wide, almost triumphal avenue. Its size was matched only by its ugliness, and it was totally out of place, not that I could imagine where its place might better be. It also appeared to be partly unfinished. The only description I could think of, as I looked at it, was that it had all the appearance of an enormous multi-storey car park crossed with a gigantic electricity substation, the only difference being that small windows lined every one of the twenty or so floors.

"That," said Bogdan, "is the Presidential palace, on which that madman, Ceaușescu, spared no expense. Inside, there is marble and gold. Outside, there is poverty and filth. No one can be surprised that we got rid of him."

He paused, and we drove on in silence.

After a while he said, almost to himself "Do you know that we were probably the only country in the Eastern bloc to use force of arms to get rid of this dictator?"

That hadn't struck me before but, on reflection, I supposed he was right, at least up to that moment. However, neither of us was in much mood for a history lesson, since we were now entering uncharted waters.

TWENTY THREE

"The world is disgracefully managed, one hardly knows to whom to complain."

Ronald Firbank, Mrs Shamefoot in *Vainglory*, 1915

Bogdan drove us to the city hall, a dark, brooding building, and parked close to what we took as the main entrance. The double doors were manned by an elderly man who could have been a cleaner or a caretaker, who was standing inside one of the doors which he was keeping fractionally open. He appeared to have appointed himself as some form of custodian, clearly preventing access to anyone of whom he did not approve. Bogdan ignored him, and simply pushed past, with me following closely. Faced with certainty rather than authority, but being unable to differentiate between the two, the door custodian let us pass, and we made our way inside, following some limited signposting which Bogdan was able to make out in the gloom.

We came to a lift, but its condition persuaded us not to take it. The door was open, but the lift floor was positioned a third of the way up the opening and, given the state of repair of much of the infrastructure that I had observed in the country already, I suggested that it might be better to take the stairs.

On the third floor, we came to an unlit wide high-ceilinged corridor, with a series of tall narrow double doors running down its length. We went to the second such door, which Bogdan was satisfied was our destination. It had some sort of title on the door on a dirty brass plaque, and inside we found a large room, with, at the far end, two ornate desks, one at either side, slightly angled towards each other. Behind each desk, illuminated by a large ornate lampstand, was a woman whom I realised was some sort of administrator or social worker. The two of them were engaged in lively conversation and barely glanced at us when we came into the room. In front of each desk were two chairs, but neither woman beckoned us to one or other of them, continuing to talk between themselves.

We stood there for several minutes while they studiously ignored us, until eventually Bogdan began speaking Romanian and went over to the right-hand desk, proffering my translated documents as he did so. The woman interjected from time to time, directing her comments as much to her colleague as to the two of us, while the other woman would respond, sometimes shaking her head, sometimes sucking her teeth, appearing to confirm her general dissatisfaction that they had been disturbed.

But there seemed, now, to be more to it. "She is saying that she and the authorities don't care for this sort of application."

As she heard Bogdan addressing me in English, she looked over at me, scowling.

"Can you explain that I am trying to rescue a child who is in dreadful circumstances?" I said.

Bogdan appeared to start, but the woman spoke over him and appeared unwilling to listen.

"Parlez-vous Français?" I asked her. She nodded briefly, looking back at the paperwork. I tried to explain that the children were in a terrible state and that I was simply trying to help by taking a child out of an institution that clearly could not care for him.

She ignored me, and continued reading, making occasional comments in Romanian.

Then suddenly, and triumphantly, she pointed to one of the documents, and announced in Romanian to Bogdan and then to me in French that 'the woman' on my marriage certificate was not the same woman whose birth certificate had been produced.

Bogdan and I were both utterly bewildered. The social worker sat back with a satisfied smile on her face and folded her arms. She announced that until that apparent contradiction had been overcome, the application to adopt the child would not proceed. She smiled across at her friend and then resumed talking to her, ignoring us both.

Bogdan took my papers off her desk and brought them over to me. "I don't understand what she is saying, but she was pointing to this red document here and then to the green one."

I looked at the papers in his hand. He was pointing to Carmel's birth certificate and to our marriage certificate. On the first of the two, there was Carmel's forename and her maiden name. On the second, the marriage certificate, her maiden name also appeared, but there, to my surprise, was another forename. On this document, she had not one, but two Christian names, Carmel Catherine. At that moment, I did not quite understand why the second Christian name should have appeared on the second document but not the first, but it was perfectly plain that she was the same person. Plain, that is, to me, but not, apparently, to the social worker, who clearly wanted to pursue any avenue to obstruct the application; and here, it seemed, at least to her satisfaction, she had been successful.

Bogdan and I beat a retreat out of the room, down the corridor, and back out into the roadway.

"You know, I have absolutely no idea why a second name should have come onto the marriage certificate, but I will have to ring home to find out what it's about because obviously, until I do, we are not going to get past that woman."

"Okay. We'll go back to my parents' apartment and we can try and place a call from their telephone."

It turned out that his parents' apartment was not that far away, since it was within Sector 1. Bogdan was able to park on the street, and he led me into a tall old apartment building, up communal stairs past some foul-smelling dustbins and into a surprisingly airy apartment, divided into a large living room, partitioned off from an equally large dining room, two bedrooms and a kitchen and bathroom.

In the living room, among an entire wall of books was a substantial radiogram, which Bogdan immediately turned on to impress me. Suddenly, the room was filled with sounds of Elton John, mournfully suggesting that some things looked better "just passing through". I shook my head at the reminder that our planet was shrinking all the time. Here we were, in post-revolutionary Romania, with all the problems and unpleasantness that I had already encountered, and the radio was broadcasting a current UK top ten hit.

However, to the telephone. Bogdan knew how to get through to the international operator given that there was no likelihood of being able to dial direct, and he found that he had to book a call, which we decided would best be made in the early evening when Carmel had returned from her shop. There was not long to wait, so we decided to stay put and review our progress.

I went through the Marriotts' checklist with him. I had, as my list required, completed my home study report and I had, within the translated documents, the necessary references, letters from our bank and from the accountant confirming my solvency, photographs of me and Carmel and of our house, and finally, a Home Office letter which confirmed the process which I was pursuing was the one approved by the UK authorities.

For his part, Bogdan was confident that we now had the mother's consent, even though it was not in writing, and we had some basic information about George's state of health when born. Obviously, there was more information on the social worker's file, and we didn't yet have an up-to-date medical report, but, hopefully, that would be obtained through some sort of medical practitioner who we now knew would be on hand from time to time at the orphanage.

Until we had those remaining documents, and until we had sorted out the current impasse with the city hall, we had to mark time. So the phone call was pretty important.

And remarkably, the call came through at the booked time, and I was able to speak to Carmel.

"We've hit a problem here because an official has noticed that when we got married, an additional Christian name was included on our certificate. Have you any idea where that came from and why it isn't on your birth certificate?"

"You silly man. You've forgotten that I'm Roman Catholic, and you probably don't know that at Confirmation, we are given a special name which we have chosen. And my chosen name was Catherine, after Kate, my mother. That's why, when we got married, I had two Christian names, but when I was born I had just the one."

"Hmm, it's not going to be terribly easy to convince this no doubt godless official, just by my telling her that. I sense that we are going to have to get this set out on some sort of declaration."

"Just tell me what to do, and I'll get hold of Tony Coltman."

Tony was a solicitor in Leamington Spa, who had already been of great assistance in preparing some of our documents, and he had told us that if we needed any logistical assistance, we should call on him immediately. In particular, he had, or had access to a telex machine, and if necessary could make immediate contact with either me, through the hotel, or with Romanian authorities, at the flick of a switch.

"OK, tell him that you need to make a statutory declaration and that it has to be notarised. Explain to him what I have told you and I'm sure that he will put that into a short document and do the necessary. The problem then, is to get it over to this country."

That indeed was the problem, since I had absolutely no idea how I could quickly get the declaration from England into the city hall in Bucharest.

"Tell you what," I said. "Ring up the man at Friendly Travel, Harry McCormick, and ask him if he has arranged any flights that are about to come over from the UK and ask him whether or not he can persuade one of his clients to bring the declaration with him, once Tony has done the honours."

Carmel promised to get on to it straight away and, of course, I knew that she would. She would ring me, she said, at the hotel, the next day, at about this time, with her progress.

So, Bogdan and I had a day to kill.

"I think we should go back to the orphanage and tell that woman that we have found the mother and that she is going to consent to an adoption. And we had better start thinking about getting a passport for him, now."

"That's not going to be so easy," I said. "Even after I've completed all the formalities, we need a visa to take us through from Romania into the UK and I doubt we'll get a passport without a visa, let alone a visa without a passport."

"We've still got to be prepared. To get a passport we need a photograph, and to get a photograph we need the child. So we'll go to the orphanage, arrange to take him out, and we'll go round to a photographic studio I know of, and at least get ready for a passport application."

***

I decided that I ought to spend the night back at Hotel Parc, so Bogdan drove me back and I had another long dribble under the shower before stretching out on the bed in an attempt to get some rest. Bogdan arranged to pick me up the next morning, and I decided that I would try and sweeten the pill for the social worker by taking some deodorant and a packet of tights for her, along with the now obligatory 200-pack carton of Kent, which Bogdan reckoned I should have on me at all times in case the need arose.

When, next morning, we arrived at the orphanage, we went straight to Ursuliano, who seemed perfectly willing to allow George out provided he was accompanied by one of his staff. He gave orders to his secretary and Bogdan and I decided to wait in the social worker's office, where we found our friend.

I went straight over to her and offered her the tights. She forced a sickly smile and turned to Bogdan. I picked up 'Multu mesc', but not much else.

"She's got his file," he said. "And there's a short report on it which shows how he came to be here in the first place."

"Let's see it then," I asked.

The social worker handed it to us. It was half a page long. Lily translated it later as part of my dossier. It contained a coldly simple narrative:

"Social Investigation, carried out at the mother's residence. Name Petre Vasilica. Address – Bucharest – number 48,

Narciselor Street, Sector II who asks for the child inclusion in the number 1 orphanage. Name of child – Petre George born on 11 V 1988.

Petre Vasilica identifies herself with identity card series S no 4870722. She was born on 3 1 1963. She works as a saleswoman at the Ilfov agriculture sector, with a wage of 2.100 lei monthly.

Out of wedlock three children aged 9, 6 and 5 have resulted.

Petre George (4th Child) is at the Doctor Cantacuzino Maternity Home.

Dwelling – a flat with three rooms with annexes, modestly furnished.

Given the condition of the above mentioned the internment of infant George into no.1 Orphanage is suggested.

Signed – Social Worker – 23 05 1988"

And that short, depressing, report effectively consigned George to the revolting establishment where I had found him. And he was approaching his third birthday, when he would face the beginnings of a downward spiral as 'incurable', to an even more unspeakable existence.

There didn't appear to be any other documentation or social enquiry report. Certainly, since the social worker had told us that the mother worked in Stanesti, there might have been some more recent communication, but there was no record of it, and, of course, it was out of date anyway. But our collection was growing.

A care worker appeared in the doorway in a cleanly pressed uniform. She was holding my foundling, who had been dressed, incongruously, in some sort of white smock.

She spoke to Bogdan who translated. She was going to accompany us out of the orphanage and was not allowed to let George out of her sight.

The four of us got into the car, and the little chap got to his feet on the rear seat, holding onto the backrest for dear life, looking out of the rear window. As we found ourselves in heavy traffic, it was clear that he had become transfixed by the movement around us and the cars following behind. He remained utterly silent.

After about five minutes, Bogdan parked against the kerb and led us to an unremarkable doorway which appeared not to have any identification on it at all. We went inside and found a bare room in which stood an ancient-looking camera on a tripod, with a rickety-looking stool in front of it. The proprietor came in from a side door, and fussed about the camera, while Bogdan again translated for me.

"He's going to take a passport photograph for us and he'll also do a photograph of the three of us if you want him to."

"Brilliant," I said. "Let's get the passport photograph done first."

This turned out to be something of a problem, because George was unable to sit up.

"No problem. I'll lie down behind the stool and hold his back up straight so that he doesn't topple over."

And so, with me lying down on the floor, with one arm on the boy's lower back and the other arm supporting the base of his neck, and doing my best to keep him as still as possible, the passport photographs were taken.

As the photographer went to his darkroom to develop the pictures, Bogdan ran to his car and got his jacket, just to improve the presentation, he said, of the tableau of the three of us. And in due course, the photographer delighted us by taking a group photograph of Bogdan, me, and our little boy. Meanwhile, the orderly who had accompanied us sat outside waiting, making inroads into the packet of Kent that I had slipped to her.

Driving back to the orphanage, George was again transfixed by the surroundings, which I realised he had never seen before. All this information was suddenly flooding into his little mind and he was observably amazed by it. When we parked at the orphanage gate, the worker picked him up and took him away from the car. As she did so, he made the first sound I had ever heard from him, no more than a squeak but nonetheless a signal of disappointment as an indication at least that he was responding to outside stimuli.

I could hardly bring myself to think that he was 'safely' back in the orphanage, but we were making headway.

We sat outside the orphanage in the ruined semicircle taking stock of our progress, which seemed, marginally, to be picking up speed. As we chatted, I realised that we were not alone. A dark-haired man, who turned out to be English, was hovering a short distance from us, listening to our conversation He introduced himself, and asked if we were having any success in our endeavours.

"Well, up to a point," I said, "but it's a struggle. At least we have identified a child, and we seem to be making headway. What about you? Have you found a child?"

"Oh yes," he said. "One, and one yet to find."

"Really? How long have you been here?"

It transpired that he had been in Bucharest for six weeks.

"I'm looking for the next child," he said.

"I don't understand. How many have you seen?"

"Oh," he said, airily, "I've looked at lots. But I haven't seen another one I like the look of yet."

I was lost for words. This wasn't a supermarket. What on earth did he think he was doing?

I shot a look at Bogdan, who seemed to be finding it harder than me to keep his temper. I got up and walked away, taking him by the elbow.

"I think we'd better leave this chap to his own business. We've got a job to do."

We left in silence and climbed into the car and sat for a moment in silence.

"I can't believe what I've just heard," Bogdan said eventually.

Another silence.

"I don't know what to say," I said. "But there will be many people who don't know where to start or how to find a child – and I'm not sure that I can judge that chap, since I don't know enough about his motives or what he can offer to the children. It's a hell of a thing."

That was pretty inadequate, but I wasn't in the mood to question the behaviour of the Englishman we had just met. I was thinking about poor George. For him, as well as the other wretches inside the orphanage, the clock was ticking.

Bogdan started the engine, and as we moved off, we snapped out of our silence.

"OK, now we have to sort out this contradictory name problem. Let's hope your lawyer can come up with an answer."

And with the help of Tony Coltman, the task proved not to be as difficult as I had first thought.

TWENTY FOUR

"If man had created man he would be ashamed of his performance."

Mark Twain, *Notebooks*, later 19th century

Carmel got through to me that evening.

"Tony has fixed the declaration, and your brilliant idea seems to be paying off. He's spoken to the travel agent and McCormick has promised to get hold of a passenger who is flying to Romania, and he'll arrange to carry it with him for you to collect. I'll find out who it is and then you can meet him at your end."

It sounded simple, and in fact it worked a treat. McCormick contacted his next client, a Welshman with, as far as I could understand it, an interest in TV aerial erection, who agreed to bring the declaration with him, and Bogdan and I set out to meet him the next afternoon.

The meeting was arranged at the Hotel Intercontinental in the centre of Bucharest, and in the early afternoon we walked into the main lobby of a different world. A uniformed doorman looked suspiciously at us, since we were at that moment conspicuously underdressed, in T-shirts and jeans, while the flow of guests and visitors in and out of the hotel lobby appeared, certainly by Romanian standards, to be smart and well-heeled. However, adopting the now well-tested self-assured look, we simply breezed past him and made our way to the hotel room where we knew Mr Evans to be staying.

The hotel corridors were clean and carpeted, the woodwork was dust free, and we could have been in any European four-star hotel. Evans came straight to the door when we knocked, ushered us in and shut the door behind us, blocking out all sound from the hotel and revealing a thoroughly comfortable and well-appointed en suite room.

"Sit down," he said, "and have a drink."

A drink? What of?

"Anything you like," he said, lifting the telephone. "Gin and tonic, whisky, Schweppes."

Speaking in English, he asked the operator for room service and, within moments, a waiter came to the door to take his order.

I shook my head in bewilderment. How come everything was on tap?

"Ah, well. This is a dollar hotel. Only dollars change hands here, and for a dollar, I can get anything."

I muttered that I would appreciate a Coke, not having had one for what seemed like an eternity. Bogdan, too, asked for a 'Pepsi'.

While we were waiting for the drinks, Mr Evans told us that he had travelled to Romania, just as I had, with the intention of adopting a baby. His strategy, however, differed starkly from mine. I had no idea how this was being arranged, but he told us that someone was going to deliver a baby to him in the hotel. Gesturing towards his luggage, he said that he had an Aids testing kit with him which would be administered on the baby, and if he liked the look of the child and the Aids test was negative, he would be leaving immediately with the baby.

Just like that.

A number of thoughts raced through my head. Who was arranging this transaction? How could he hope to get through British border controls? Who was to administer the Aids test? Had he not heard that such tests on babies were, apparently, notoriously unreliable? Was he not going to see anything of Romania? Was he not to have any idea at all about the country that the baby was leaving? Did the baby have one or two parents? Was the child being taken from their home or from an orphanage?

The questions tumbled into my head and rushed around my mind in such chaos that I found myself unable to articulate any of them. This extraordinary visit appeared to be hermetically sealed from the reality of this country. Evans had left the UK and arrived in this Western-style hotel with only the briefest of glimpses of the real Romania through his taxi window on the way from the airport. He would only venture out of his hotel room on checking out, would climb back into his taxi and then return to the UK. I felt utterly bewildered and it was clear, too, that Bogdan shared my surprise. At that moment, I felt a stirring of sympathy for the view that perhaps the removal of the child in such circumstances had a number of unsatisfactory undertones.

My thoughts were interrupted by a knock on the door, and the waiter reappeared with the drinks, the Cokes for me and Bogdan, and a whisky on the rocks for Evans, who handed out the drinks to the two of us.

"Now, let me just dig out the envelope that I brought over for you," he said, ferreting in a briefcase. Sure enough, he found and handed over a large foolscap envelope. A quick look inside reassured me that it was what I expected, a statutory declaration, signed by Carmel, witnessed, and with a further endorsement by a Notary Public. Good old Tony Coltman!

Bogdan and I made small talk for a moment but neither he nor I felt comfortable in that room, partly because of the stark contrast with the surrounding city and partly because of Evans's remarkable tale, so we made our excuses and left.

On the way back to the car, I found it difficult to articulate my thoughts.

"Well, at least we've got that statutory declaration, and we can go back to the town hall with it."

"OK," said Bogdan, seemingly deep in thought. I wondered what he made of the contrast which we had just encountered, but I kept my questions to myself. Life must have been confusing enough for Romanians without having to attempt to make head or tail of dollar hotels on the one hand and poverty on the other.

We had time enough to go back to his parents' apartment, pick up my documents, and get back to the town hall, and within the hour, we found ourselves back in front of those double doors. Once more, they were ajar, and we entered, finding the scene completely unchanged from that which we had left a couple of days before. There were the two social workers, engaged in lively conversation across the room from their respective desks. No one else was in the room and indeed they appeared to have nothing else to do.

The one to whom Bogdan had spoken on the previous occasion looked over at us without offering any form of greeting. Bogdan went across the room and put the documents back on the table in front of her, together, this time, with the statutory declaration. She took only the briefest of moments to look at the documents and appeared to recognise them immediately.

She started speaking to Bogdan with what looked uncomfortably like a leer on her face. She finished what she was saying with something of a laugh, and again sat back, folding her arms.

For once, Bogdan appeared lost for words. He picked up the documents and put them all into the envelope holding the statutory declaration and turned to me.

"She says the law has changed. We're too late. There will be no adoptions, now, until the new government is elected and a new presidency appointed and she says that she's got no idea when that will be."

He and I turned on our heels and left that room, watched by the two women. I almost imagined that I could hear them sniggering as we shut the doors behind us.

"What on earth are we going to do now?" For once, Bogdan was asking me for advice.

I needed to think. What, indeed, were we to do?

"Why don't we go to the parliament building and find out whether she is telling the truth?" I said. "After all, up until now, it appears that the President has had to sign off all international adoptions, so where better to ask?"

In fact, parliament was within walking distance, and so we walked through to the large square in front of the parliament, past the sentries who were standing at attention at equidistant points, fully armed and no doubt most uncomfortable in the heat, facing outwards, gazing over the heads of passers by.

Despite the presence of armed guards, we were not challenged in any way as we walked into the main entrance of the building. Within moments, we found our way to an inner chamber where, remarkably, I found myself facing a high-ranking official who spoke perfect English. Whether he was a councillor, the mayor or a member of parliament in the strictest term, was neither clear nor relevant for, of course, I reflected, there had been no elections. But he did, in any event, appear to be someone who had exercised authority in the aftermath of the execution of Ceauşescu.

I recounted the now familiar mantra to him, and told him of the latest obstacle which had been presented to us at the town hall.

"The social worker was right up to a point," he replied, in flawless English. "It's not that the law has changed, it's more that parliament has now dissolved, and it is not possible to nominate or identify a President who has the authority to sign any papers to release a child from the country. After Ceauşescu was removed, it was generally agreed that parliament should sit for six months as some form of interim government, but that six months is now up. We have to hold elections before we can properly call ourselves a law-making body and before we can identify a President to complete the adoption process. In fact, it may all change anyway, because we really need legislation to deal with these things."

He was polite but matter of fact, and it was perfectly clear that there was nothing more to be said. On the face of it, we were completely stuck.

What now? Bogdan and I retreated, the two of us feeling pretty bruised by these latest developments. We pondered what other avenues we might follow – surely the country would not grind to a halt just because parliament had dissolved?

"So, we won't get any help from either a mayor or a President, but that always seemed a bit dodgy to me in the first place. Why don't we take some legal advice from the horse's mouth?"

"What's this about a horse?"

"When we say 'the horse's mouth', we mean getting information from the original source – heaven knows where the saying comes from, but there it is."

"You don't say."

"Yup, I do say," I said with a grin, "so let's find a real lawyer."

"A real lawyer?"

"I mean, let's go find a judge."

And we retraced our steps to his car.

***

Bogdan drove to the central courts, a large building in dark stone, full of gargoyles and turrets, set behind a pattern of tree-lined streets on which we found a parking space.

Perhaps European law courts are all the same, but I confess that there was a passing resemblance to the Royal Courts on the Strand in London, and I felt almost at home.

We walked through wide hallways and the ever-present bustle of legal activity and we were directed, ultimately, to a corridor on to which a series of doors opened, with nameplates on each. Bogdan found his way to one, which he said was a district judge.

The door was open, and we entered a comparatively cramped room, dominated by a large desk and several filing cabinets. Behind the desk, in shirt sleeves, attending to paperwork with an impressively large fountain pen, was a white-haired well-fed-looking man who greeted us with a cheerful smile. Bogdan introduced us in Romanian and then I asked him if he spoke French.

He said he did but that his language skills were comparatively rusty. Once I explained that mine were no better, the two of us relaxed into a conversation about the comparison between the English and Romanian legal codes, the status of judge and the appeals procedures.

"But why, particularly, have you come to see me?" he asked

I explained that we were facing some difficulty with the adoption process, because parliament had dissolved.

He nodded. "That's right, and until elections are held and we have a properly functioning parliament, law-making will stand still."

But what about the law of adoption, I asked. The idea that a child is found, the mayor approves, and the President signs off the adoption certificate seemed, at the least, to be artificial.

"That's perfectly true," he said. "And since there are going to be a lot of these adoptions, we need a proper law of adoption, not just to satisfy ourselves, but to satisfy the countries where the children go."

I asked him what influence the judges would bring to bear on any adoption reform.

"Quite a lot," he said. "You can imagine that parliament is likely to be faced with an enormous number of laws which must be made following the departure of dear Ceauşescu. So any help they can get from judges is likely to be very important. But we don't have any committees or other organisation that can advise the judges while we try to advise parliament."

I wondered if he might appreciate an outline of the law in England. I was anxious not to appear patronising, but I thought that perhaps a working model of adoption law in England might form the basis of discussions by the judges in Romania.

To my surprise, he jumped at the idea.

"Okay," I said, without knowing quite where it would take us, "I'll get hold of a copy of our most recent Adoption Act and I will fax it over to Bogdan, here, and he'll pass it on to you."

He said he would look forward to it and he rose from his seat and shook us both warmly by the hand, wishing us a cheery 'au revoir'.

As we made our way out of the complex and back to the car, I said to Bogdan, "We may have an ally there. I think that even if parliament isn't functioning for the time being, there must be a way of carrying out a legal adoption, and if we can, that judge may well be a useful gatekeeper."

"I think you're right. If you can get hold of that Act of Parliament and get it to me, I'll get it to him and hopefully he'll help us."

Certainly, we had suffered two backward steps, but maybe, just maybe, this was one step forward once more.

TWENTY FIVE

"The world is quickly bored by the recital of
misfortunes, and willingly avoids the sight of distress."

Somerset Maugham, *The Moon and Sixpence*, 1919

The next day, we discovered that the doctor who
had overall responsibility for the orphanage was on
duty. Bogdan and I found our way to her office and
discovered a young woman who had all the appearance of a
clinician that Ursuliano lacked. In particular, it was pretty
clear that she was distinctly unhappy about the condition
of the children under her care, and just as frustrated by her
inability to do very much for them.

However, Bogdan was able to show her the translated
BAAF medical form, and she completed it immediately, en-
abling us to take it over to Lily for translation. When that task
had been completed, I judged that it was time to meet Kirsty
Rowe once more, so I telephoned and made an appointment.

When I arrived, her whole demeanour suggested that I
was not welcome.

I set out my stall as plainly as I could. "I've found a
child and, believe me, he is in a pretty poor state, given
the surroundings in which he is living. The orphanage

has identified him as free for adoption, and the mother has already been approached and has indicated that she consents. As you know, I have attempted to avoid further delay by ensuring that instead of undergoing a home study examination after visiting the orphanage, I ensured that that was done to the satisfaction of my local authority and the adoption panel before I first came out. Can I assume, therefore, since the department already has that report, that it won't in fact be necessary for me to return to England, since there is nothing I can do there?"

"I'm afraid that you will have to follow the procedure. That means returning to England."

"But what on earth for? All the documents which have to be prepared in England have been prepared already. I've obtained the necessary medical report on the BAAF form. As I understand it, the embassy sends that back to London, and all then that London has to do is to confirm to its own satisfaction that the necessary formalities have fallen into place, so that the Home Office can be assured that an entry clearance can be given."

"That makes no difference to the procedure. You cannot take the child from the orphanage, let alone from Romania, until entry clearance has been given, and that clearance is given not by us but by London."

"I know that, but what is the point of my being there for that purpose?"

"It is procedure."

"Look," I said, "I doubt you have been inside any of these orphanages, but I can assure you that they are perfectly dreadful. To endure that lack of care for one day longer, let alone a week or, by the sound of it, even more than that, is positively harmful to all the children and in particular to the child whom I have identified. Don't you see how important it is to me to get him out?"

"I'm sorry to say that individual cases cannot be considered. You have to return to England and await Home Office permission before the child can be removed."

I asked if I could see the Consul.

"He will give you exactly the same answer," she said, but when I pressed her again, she agreed to have a word with him.

I waited outside her office, sitting on a settee in a grand hallway, furnished in a style which seemed closer to the British Raj than to Eastern Europe. The Consul, who I knew to be one Bob Howe, emerged from a side door with the vice consul.

"Miss Rowe has told me about your discussion. I'm afraid that she is right. There is a protocol which we have to observe, and there can be no exceptions. The fact that you obtained a home study report before you travelled to Romania makes no difference. You have to return to England."

There was the faintest suspicion of a smirk on the Vice Consul's face as I accepted defeat. I left the medical report and a copy of the birth certificate with them both and asked them to send them to the Department of Health in London, before leaving the embassy feeling utterly frustrated.

I hadn't told them of my discovery that the law had either changed or that, somehow, it had gone up in smoke – they would know that sooner rather than later in any event. For the moment, I had to sort out with Bogdan exactly what our next steps would have to be.

TWENTY SIX

"The moment we care for anything deeply, the world –
that is, all the other miscellaneous interests – becomes
our enemy."

G.K. Chesterton, *Heretics*, 1905

In fact, Bogdan was busy making his own plans while I
was at the embassy. While he had no legal training, he
had taken quite a shine to the district judge whom we
had met at the law courts and he, for his part, seemed more
than willing to talk about adoption.

After I left the Vice Consul's office, Bogdan and I met
up and he told me of his plans.

"That judge says that I can present an application to
adopt the child on your behalf. He says that if the mother
agrees, I can make an application for a Romanian adoption
order, provided I have the permission of both you and your
wife to take the case on your behalf."

"Really?"

"Look, I already have the mother's agreement. All
I need to do is to bring her to the court and make an
application before the judges for an order, and, how do
you say, 'Bingo', I can get an order. We don't need the

President's signature or anything like that – we'll have an adoption order."

"But how do you know what to say or what to ask for? There are probably forms to complete and applications to lodge at the court."

"That's no problem. That judge really does want to help, and he has promised to guide me through the procedure."

What an extraordinary twist. On the one hand, the town hall had effectively brought the shutters down, and the President was no longer in a position to sign off any form of adoption declaration in the way the Marriotts had suggested. Yet, as Bogdan had said, when we couldn't get in the door we would climb through the window, and this particular window seemed to lead us to an apparently uncomplicated legal process. It didn't overcome the problem that an English court would not recognise a Romanian adoption, but at least it would be a start, and Bogdan seemed so enthused with the idea that it seemed churlish to suggest that there might be any difficulty.

I told him of my meeting with the Vice Consul and that I was going to have to go back to England.

"That's no problem. Make sure that you and Carmel give me your power of attorney, and I'll start the adoption process while you are over there. To keep him on our side, I've promised the judge that I will pass him the Adoption Act that you discussed with him, even though that won't do much for our own application – the only problem is how we actually get a copy."

"Ah, I reckon we can use that wonderful invention, the fax machine," I said.

"But where are we going to find one?"

"I think I'll ask the British embassy if I can pass it through their fax machine as a gesture of co-operation with the Romanian people."

"Wow. Do you reckon they'll wear that?"

"I have my doubts, but on the other hand, it's no skin off their nose."

So, knowing that I had to return to England, we decided that I would take the next plane out, and I would batter away at the British authorities while Bogdan would go about his business as our advocate in the Bucharest law courts. And I would fax him a power of attorney signed by both Carmel and me, as soon as I got home.

TWENTY SEVEN

"Do not go gentle into that good night,
Old age should burn and rave at close of day;
Rage, rage against the dying of the light."

Dylan Thomas, 1914–53

And so I had to obey 'procedure' and return to England. The night before I left, I met Bogdan's parents for the first time. His father, a tall, erect engineer, who, like his wife spoke nothing other than Romanian, and his mother, a perfectly charming lady with the kindest face. Bogdan had told them all about our adventures and about the state of the orphanage, and without hesitation they both insisted that when I returned, I should stay with them, and meanwhile they would do their best to provide some daily comfort for George.

But as I left, all optimism evaporated. Did I really know what I was doing? Certainly, there had been some forward movement, but at each junction I was being knocked back. The Romanian authorities, in the main, appeared indifferent to the plight of the 'orphans' and hostile to the idea of removal abroad, albeit into a family life. The British seemed hardly any better.

I stared gloomily out of the aeroplane window as the airliner took off for London. All I had to show for my endeavours over the past weeks was a tiny picture of this waif-like figure which might ultimately be his passport photograph. I had no other documents to identify either the child or my endeavour to adopt him.

I wanted to get home, to the comfort of my home and my wife, and to unload this increasing burden of both fury and depression – fury that at a distance not much greater than that between London and Aberdeen, the good burghers of Vienna were indulging themselves in expensive cafés with rich coffee and tasty patisserie while children in Bucharest, just six hundred miles away, and indeed throughout Romania, were abandoned and given barely enough food to survive. Depression itself was not something I had encountered before I embarked on this trip – but now, for the first time in my life, I was experiencing waves of helplessness and anxiety.

I got home, and Carmel and I each took a kitchen chair and sat out in the garden under the washing line trying to make sense of what I had just been through. As best I could, I retraced my steps through Bacau and Bucharest, telling her about the pollution, the poverty, the disgusting state of the two orphanages which I had visited, the apparent corruption, and the extraordinary gulf between the rich – those who had access to hard currency – and the poor, who did not. I told her of the unhelpful behaviour of the British consulate staff, my meeting with Bogdan, his delightful parents and my surprise at the lack of knowledge, within at least their circle of Romanian society, of the appalling conditions in the hundreds of orphanages around their country. When it came to describing my first visit to Orphanage Number One, and recalling the little squint-eyed, red-haired, boy standing wailing at the door, I finally succumbed to quite uncontrollable tears.

There was little that Carmel could say or do in the face of my distress, other than sit and listen and hold my hand. The cool, impossibly green English evening seemed an eternity away from the dust of the orphanage yard. The world was upside down, and at that moment, I felt powerless to right it. But gradually the sobs subsided, as I pulled myself together, concentrating on telling her of the next steps that I had to take.

"Don't despair," she said. "You have found him and I know that you will get him out. After a decent night's sleep, you will feel stronger. You know that in every step of the way along this difficult path you have my full support. I only wish I could be with you."

Of course, I couldn't sleep. As I attempted to relax in my home, I took in my surroundings with a new eye. I was surrounded by so much that I took for granted: toothpaste in the morning to brush my teeth, food on the table at breakfast, fresh milk, delivered to the door in whatever quantities and at whatever frequency I might dictate. Driving to the rail station along roads without suspension-crunching potholes, commuting into work on clean rolling stock. Walking the last half mile or so in Birmingham city centre without the acrid taste of exhaust fumes caking my throat, breathing air which, by comparison with Bucharest, was positively mountain fresh.

I sat by my tape deck and recorded a lengthy letter to my brothers in New Zealand, keeping them abreast of my endeavours. They later told me that I sounded so dreadful that they seriously considered advising me not to go any further.

But, of course, as I reflected, deep into my first night back home, I had in fact made substantial headway and gradually my spirits rose. Despite the obstacles placed in my path by both the Romanian and British authorities, I had managed to identify a child who could be brought out of an orphanage. Not only that, but Bogdan, bless him, had promised that he and his parents would visit every day to ensure that even in small quantities, they would provide better sustenance for him, and give him some comfort for part of the long-abandoned days that he had to endure in that perfectly dreadful place.

And, of course, Bogdan had that most precious of documents, his birth certificate, precious, that is, because, as he had assured me a second time just before I left, in the absence of an identity card which of course the poor child did not have, that was his one and vitally important identity document, without which the state would probably not be able, without greater effort, to either deal with or dispose of him. There was, of course, no guarantee, but it seemed reasonable enough to me that given the antipathy shown towards him in the orphanage and the failure of anybody to seek him out as a potential adoptee, he would not be going anywhere within the next few weeks, while I endeavoured to complete a plan to have him adopted, released, and brought into this country.

So, what now? Somehow, Bogdan and I had to kick-start the international adoption process in the absence of any current law which would be observed by either the Romanian state or the British authorities. There was no way that, in my view, the child could survive in the orphanage for months to come while a new parliament ground out the preparation and approval of a new raft of the necessary legislation. The friendly judge whom Bogdan and I had found in the Bucharest law courts had indicated a willingness, even an eagerness, to digest the current United Kingdom legislation if I could somehow get it to him, and had he not told me that he would be delighted to consider it and proffer it as a model which the new law-makers in Bucharest might wish to consider? He at least was on our side, and even if, in the cold light of day, it seemed a hopeless idea, I decided that anything and everything was worth a try. So, on my first evening back at work, I visited our library and took out a copy of the 1976 Adoption Act.

And then to Bob Edwards, my wife's accountant. He had known of my proposed trip to Romania, given that he had signed a certificate of solvency for us, and had told me that if there was anything he could do, I should only ask. So, feeling slightly guilty, never having been one to hold people to such promises, I rang him.

"Bob," I said. "I need to copy a statute and transmit it over to Romania and try, somehow, to persuade the powers that be that our adoption legislation might well form a helpful basis for legislation which at the moment they simply do not have."

He asked me how he could help.

"I have the fax number of the British embassy and, potty as it sounds, I want to transmit an Act of Parliament to the embassy, have it collected by a contact I have over there and he will pass it to a family judge."

I could imagine Bob's face.

"Can't you send it?"

"I would if I had any confidence in the postal service over there, but I sent a letter to a doctor a month ago and it still hasn't arrived, and time is precious."

"It'll take all night, you know," he said. I sensed that he was trying hard not to laugh.

"Ah," I replied, conspiratorially. "It's one of a number of avenues that I simply have to follow, and although the embassy will probably not welcome an enormous document coming through the fax machine, with the letter that I've prepared, I hope that they'll agree to act as a conduit."

"Come along, then, to my office, and we'll get to work."

And so, late into the night of my second night home, I laboured over Bob's fax machine and transmitted page after page of adoption legislation to the embassy, explaining and confirming again in a covering letter why it was that they were presented with this statute and who would be collecting it. As far as I knew, once a document had been transmitted by a fax machine to another, the receiving station would simply follow the instruction, and print the facsimile. I very much doubted that my ruse would be welcomed by embassy staff, just as I realised that I was requiring the receiving fax machine to use a very great deal of paper, a commodity which was, as far as I could establish, not the most immediately available in Bucharest.

But it did not need a great deal of soul-searching to justify what I was doing, and although I could not view this as a victory of any size, the fact that I was doing something constructive helped to lighten my mood.

Bogdan, for his part, promised that he would pick up the paperwork as soon as it arrived and he would get on with this task of trying to adopt George. Frankly, I had to admit to a number of doubts on that front. But then again, even if the legal process got nowhere, he would nonetheless be able to produce the necessary consent from the mother to satisfy the Romanian and British authorities and to allow the orphanage to release the child. So I left him to it while I addressed equally pressing things in the UK.

***

I knew that I had to contact the Department of Health and try and make some sense of the sequence that the paperwork and Kirsty Rowe had insisted I follow. Not only had she told me, but I had read, both in the Marriotts' advice and on the paperwork received from the Department of Health that I would not get the infant out of the orphanage, let alone into the United Kingdom, without the increasingly, at least in my eyes, unattainable entry clearance. Then I needed a visa. The clearance would come from London, while the visa was issued by the embassy. And the embassy would not move one centimetre forward without the nod from London.

The main point of attack would now obviously have to be in London, given that Kirsty Rowe had already made it plain that there was nothing more the embassy would or could do until Home Office entry clearance was received, and both of us knew that the Home Office would do nothing without the approval of the Department of Health.

And Kirsty Rowe had underlined Home Office insistence that the orphanage was not to release the child until entry clearance had been given.

The one advantage about my being sent back to England to continue the process was that I could pursue the relevant officials without having to rely on the assistance of the international telephone operator. So, back to the telephone I went. I had the name of the first person with whom I should make contact at the Home Office immigration department, which appeared to nestle somewhere in the Elephant and Castle area of London.

An apt name, I thought, as I waited interminably on my umpteenth call. The hide of an elephant and the immovability of a castle.

***

The next step had to be to convince the Department of Health, who, I knew, needed the child's medical history. That, thankfully, was set out on the BAAF form and that had been completed by the paediatrician in Bucharest, translated from Romanian by Lily, and had now been sent on, I hoped, by the embassy. The home study report had already been completed, which I thought was an advantage, since it seemed to be accepted that prospective adopters were expected to leave that particularly important part of the process, albeit on DHSS advice, until after they had identified a child. All these documents had been transmitted to London by the local authority before I had left England.

Over the next few days and gradually, but to me, achingly slowly, I managed to ascend what appeared to be an interminable ladder, speaking to one and then another civil servant, and explaining my case at each time and to each new voice.

No one, of course, had the slightest interest in my history. Nor did they have any inclination to either listen to or understand the ghastly difficulties faced by the children in those orphanages. I was, I had to recognise, just another citizen trying to wriggle through the numerous hoops presented by United Kingdom immigration legislation, to sneak another unwanted entrant into England, where the welfare system was already struggling to meet the needs of its indigenous population.

My only weapon, at this stage, was stubbornness. I was not to be put off or deflected, and there were days when I put through as many as five calls to the Department of Health, insisting, each time, that I be given the name of the person to whom I was speaking and insisting, too, that they, equally, were aware of the subject matter of my call.

I explained over and over again that I had approval from my local authority to adopt not one but two children, and that I had been promised co-operation at the highest level by the then Secretary of State for Health. While that was not strictly true, these were desperate times, and if I could drop a name, however tangentially, it might just help move my case centimetre by centimetre along the corridors which I imagined snaked through the grey bleakness of the aptly named Lunar House.

Obviously, none of the officials who took my calls had the faintest idea of the horrors which I had observed. And so I felt I had to tell them. I refined my description to a succinct and, in my view, hard-hitting summary which I would always end by making it plain that I felt it was now my duty to ensure that George should not have to endure his plight for one hour longer than was absolutely necessary. Every hour which passed, I repeated, caused him further damage and they could rest assured that I would not desist from contacting the department on a daily, if not hourly, basis and I would when necessary take my case to the highest authority (whatever I imagined that meant).

Then, one Friday morning in mid August, after yet another volley of small-arms fire at the hapless civil servant on the other end of the line, I seemed to hear, in my increasingly fevered imagination, another bolt being withdrawn on the door which remained stubbornly closed. But if I had detected a sense of reluctant co-operation, it was to be blown away.

I was asked, again, to provide a medical certificate for the child. Of course, I had done so, and would they please look again at the file. There was a pause.

"Ah, yes. Well, what about a Romanian social work report?" asked my interrogator. The urge to ask whether he was winding me up was almost overwhelming. But I maintained as much calm as I could.

"You probably don't realise how poor the social work resources are in that country," I said. "Sure, they have social workers but they are terribly thin on the ground and the whole question of a welfare service is, I'm afraid, laughable. If it were otherwise, and the government could afford social workers, it could afford not to keep the children in these ghastly institutions. But anyway, I'll think you'll find that a social work report from Romania isn't on your checklist; what you do need is a home study report from my local authority rather than one in Romania, and if you look at my file, you'll see that one has been prepared and approved by the Warwickshire adoption panel."

Again, I went through what was now a familiar mantra. I could not leave this child in this orphanage a moment longer and I insisted that the department stop erecting new obstacles as some sort of delaying tactic. I had done everything asked of me. I had submitted to a home study report by my local authority, which had, through its adoption panel, agreed that I and my wife were fit persons to adopt two children from Romania. Carmel and I had been subjected to medical and financial examinations and had passed muster. I had completed all the necessary government paperwork through the Romanian embassy and I had visited the country and identified a child. The child appeared physically well, although dreadfully delayed, and not a moment more was to be lost. I had complied to the letter with the guidance set out on the curiously labelled RON 117, and could do no more. The ball was very firmly in their court.

I needed entry clearance before the British consulate would provide me with a visa, and I had, as I explained into the phone, the uneasy impression that I was being bounced between the two of them. They should be talking to each other and probably were, but were being of no assistance to me, a British citizen, as a result. Gritting my teeth, I explained that I knew very well and did not need to be told that international adoptions were still very much the exception, and I quite understood that procedures had to be observed and protocols followed. However, while civil servants scratched their chins and gave the lowest priority to children in Romania, the damage that those children had already suffered would be magnified.

Then, a bombshell. "We require confirmation that while the child was in the orphanage he was never visited by anyone and that he never left the orphanage at any time."

Where on earth did that one come from?

"You're not serious."

"That is a requirement of this department before we can recommend to the Home Office that entry be permitted."

"But it's obvious," I protested. "The child was abandoned. You've seen the social enquiry report which put him there in the first place. That, for heaven's sake, was when he was 10 days old. And he's been there ever since."

The voice on the other end of the phone never wavered. "That information must be passed in the form of a letter or other confirmation from the orphanage, and until it has been produced, we can take your application no further."

"Look. Nothing of this kind was mentioned by the embassy, and I was told simply to return to England. I set out all the documents which were required, and those which had not already been sent to the department in London were handed over to the Vice Consul. I am now three thousand miles away from the orphanage, and the likelihood of my being able to get hold of the sort of declaration which you have just announced in anything under many months from now is remote. The postal service is haphazard, and the orphanage has other things to attend to."

I was, as I spoke, wondering just how remote from reality these people were. Did they imagine that parents, family, friends would make arrangements to take the infants out for tea or have them to stay from time to time? Or was this, as I suspected it was, just another obstacle thrown in my path, and no doubt those of other aspiring adopters, by a government desperate to limit the influx of these children?

"I'm afraid that the state of the postal service is not something that we can take into account. You need to be aware of the department's requirements. No doubt you will inform us when you have the necessary information."

"Well, thanks a million," I muttered as I rang off. How many more hurdles were going to be presented by these people? I wondered, between waves of despair. I could see any request being delayed in the post for months, given the non-arrival of my letter to Sadovici, and even on arrival, could I really imagine that the orphanage would prepare such a nonsense letter and return it? It would be quicker for me to fly to Romania and present the request myself, have it translated, take it to the embassy and then fly back.

***

I got home that night and immediately phoned Bogdan and gave him the news of this latest development. But he didn't seem fazed by it at all.

"No problem. I'll drop by the orphanage tomorrow, and get a letter which confirms that, and I'll drop it straight in to Lily and then the embassy. What do you think the Kent are for?"

Of course, I had left him with several hundred Kent, in case of 'eventualities', and despite any misgivings about the graft that this exposed, jumping whatever queue there might be with a few cigarettes seemed a reasonable step to take in the face of the intransigence which I was experiencing in England.

In fact it took two days, but on the 14th August I received a telex from Bogdan via Tony Coltman:

TODAY I LEFT THE EMBASSY THE CERTIFICATE THAT GEORGE NEVER LEFT THE ORPHANAGE AND WAS NEVER VISITED BY ANYONE. I LEFT IT TODAY (TUESDAY) BECAUSE DOCTOR URSULIANO WAS ON HOLIDAY TILL MONDAY. I COULDN'T HAND IT IN PERSON TO MRS ROWE BECAUSE SHE WOULD NOT SEE ME…

And then mysteriously … WITH THE ROMANIAN EVERYTHING IS OK AND I'M WAITING FOR THE 24 TH AUGUST TO GET THE DECISION.

So, Kirsty Rowe had refused to see Bogdan. In my fury, I

imagined that she, like I, had overlooked the fact that I continued to have help in Romania and that the certificate, far from being an impossibility, was a matter of such simplicity. Perhaps I was being unfair, and she was not being obstructive, but all my dealings with her and the department seemed to point in the other direction. In any event, she couldn't deny that the request for the certificate, however much it had arrived late and out of left field, had now been complied with. And the 'decision'? I reckoned that that must relate to Bogdan's application for an adoption order. That, however, didn't affect the need for entry clearance.

So I renewed my telephonic onslaught with increasing energy, and again found myself locked into something akin to a revolving door.

***

On the Friday after I had received Bogdan's telex, and after daily calls to the department, the door appeared, at last, to creak open. With what seemed quite unnecessary reluctance on their part, I was given the news I desperately sought. It was likely that I would, after all, be given entry clearance, and that confirmation would be likely on the following Monday. Both I and the consulate, I was told, would be informed.

But my experiences prompted me to remain cautious. Just as before, I asked for the name and department of the person to whom I was speaking.

"Mr Brunskill."

"And when should I telephone you on Monday for

confirmation that entry clearance will be forthcoming?"

"In the morning, any time after 9am," said Mr Brunskill.

"I'm very grateful to you," I said. "I will ring you on Monday morning."

I replaced the receiver with new hope. The continuing and dispiriting grind of one step forward and two steps back might now just be reversing itself. But I was not so suffused with confidence that I could tell either Carmel or Bogdan of this development and I kept it to myself over the weekend, barely able to concentrate on anything else.

On Monday the 20th August, barely able to exercise patience, and anxious not to hassle Brunskill, I waited until 9.30am, then picked up the phone and dialled the now familiar number.

I gave the department I needed and the specific extension of Mr Brunskill.

There was no answer and the telephone simply dialled out.

I rang again and spoke to the main switchboard and asked for the department but gave no extension. The phone was answered by a young man to whom I had never spoken before.

"Good morning. I wonder if you would be kind enough to put me through to Mr Brunskill? I spoke to him on Friday and he is expecting my call."

"That's not possible, Sir. Mr Brunskill is now on annual leave."

TWENTY EIGHT

"I am in earnest – I will not equivocate – I will not excuse
– I will not retreat a single inch – and I will be heard!"

William Lloyd Garrison, *Salutatory
Address of the Liberator*, 1 January 1831

"I'm sorry," I stuttered, "there must be some mistake."

"In what way, Sir?"

"We spoke on Friday. I am to ring him today for an update, for confirmation… for a conclusion."

A pause.

"I have the department diary in front of me, Sir. It confirms that the last day of work before Mr Brunskill's annual leave was last Friday."

Another pause while I fought to gather my thoughts

A hint of impatience. "Can I be of any further assistance?"

I tried to focus. "Well, yes, you can. You can identify and connect me to his superior."

Silence.

"I'm not sure that I'm free to do that, Sir."

"Look," I said, "I can accept that this is not your

doing, and that it is unfair to shoot the messenger, but I assure you that if I am prevented from climbing the chain of command, then I will descend it." I wondered for a moment where was I getting sentences like this from, but I was so fired up I didn't much care.

"By that I mean that I will start with the Minister and come downward, as directed. Eventually I will land on Brunskill's manager. I don't care for confrontation but you might sense the way this is going."

Another pause.

"Sir, you probably realise that I am not familiar with your file. I'm going to have to ask you to hold the line while I find a way to the next step which I hope will be acceptable to both parties."

Both parties? I didn't want this to develop into 'us' and 'you'. I just wanted that door to open.

"OK. I'm grateful for any endeavour, and I'm happy to hold."

So, hold I did. Filling in my contact with more information from time to time as he sought clarification as before, of my life history, the Universe and Everything. There was no point in losing my temper, although I was seething at my treatment: I needed co-operation, and my locker was pretty bare. Ranting and raving were securely locked away in a box marked Emergency Only.

My patience bore fruit. I was finally put through to someone who I imagined inhabited the next level, Donna Sidonio, who, although polite, required me, again, to start from square one – Virginia Bottomley, my local authority head of services, the home study report, adoption approval, arrival in Bucharest, the state of the orphanages, the demands of the British embassy. And now this.

"From whatever angle you look at this, the taxpayer, the adoptive parents, fairness, but above all, this poor infant, stuck in a urine-soaked cot, the behaviour of this agency of government isn't what I and maybe you might be entitled to expect."

That sounded pretty pompous, but it ranked a little higher than "how dare you treat the citizen in this fashion". I had to keep Sidonio onside if I could. If she shut down the conversation I really couldn't immediately identify my next step.

"I can see that you have been having something of a hard time."

"You're right," I said. "But I must have this sorted out – not at some vague future time but yesterday. Believe me, the child is facing removal from this orphanage as 'incurable'. Not because he is, but because he is now in his third year of life, and I am assured that around his third birthday he will be removed from one level of sewer to another, lower level. I cannot allow that to happen. And I need your help – help which at the moment seems to be as far away as ever."

"Look," she said, "I'll get to the bottom of this and find out what has happened to the entry clearance. Can I ask you to leave it with me? I'll have my assistant contact you with news, hopefully within the course of today."

There wasn't much more I could ask, so I thanked her and rang off. But as every minute passed, I became more and more anxious. I couldn't get the image of that revolting gruel being pumped into his stomach out of my head, of his palpable distress, and the dreadful smell of human excrement. But while I couldn't rest, a small voice at the back of my mind kept reminding me that none of the civil servants had any idea of the plight of the child whom Carmel and I had now named.

We had done so as soon as I got over my immediate distress on my return from Bucharest. I had a copy of this passport photograph and I passed it over to Carmel, wondering what she might make of his little face.

"He's Dominic," she declared. "Look at his lovely dark hair and his beautiful eyes. St Dominic – all Dominicans – are dark and handsome, and that should be his name."

So that was that. I felt that he should keep his Romanian name, while we would christen him with both that name and Dominic. Coincidentally, he would have the same name as the young nurse in Bucharest. I was delighted; I loved the name and it was obvious that Carmel had fallen in love with the child in the picture. So I had to get Dominic out of that place.

***

That afternoon, I did receive the promised phone call and even an apology. I was assured that it was entirely probable that the department would be passing the necessary formal approval to the Home Office within the next couple of days and they, that is the Home Office, in the person of a Mike Lyne or his assistant, a Mrs McCluskey, would be contacting me with formal confirmation.

Now, at last, I felt I could tell Carmel and I could arrange my flight back to Bucharest. There was, I found, room on a flight leaving on Sunday from Heathrow, and the ever helpful Mr McCormick promised to have a ticket waiting for me at the airport. For once, I assumed that things were going my way and I took it that I would be receiving the promised call. I rang Bogdan and gave him the news – he sounded delighted and promised to meet me at the airport.

My new-found optimism was justified. On Thursday, Mr Lyne telephoned as promised and he confirmed that the Home Office had received the necessary checks and authorisations from the Department of Health, and he told me, a little unnecessarily I thought, that the Home Secretary 'saw no reason to deny entry' to Dominic.

However, I ignored the civil-service-speak, and thanked him effusively. He assured me that the necessary telex would be in the hands of the embassy by the following day.

"I'm flying out on Sunday. I'll contact the Vice Consul on Monday and hopefully complete all the formalities at that end very quickly so that I can get the child back to England."

"Good luck. If there's any problem, do contact me or my assistant, Mrs McCluskey."

I thanked him again, not imagining that there could possibly be any more obstacles. But I wrote their names down just to be on the safe side.

Had I thought about it, I would have remembered that Bogdan had spoken of Friday 24th August, as the day of 'the decision'. But I was too taken up with the arrangements which I was having to rush through to think about that. Instead, I set about collecting the necessary supplies and begging more time away from court in readiness for what I hoped would be the final chapter.

TWENTY NINE

"The lunatic's visions of horror are all drawn from the material of daily fact."

William James, *Varieties of Religious Experience*, 1902

On this Sunday afternoon, I flew into Bucharest with a slightly different payload. I still had my rucksack, full once more with cartons of Kent, bars of soap, toothpaste, and even washing-up liquid for Bogdan's parents, and some perfume for his mother. And a selection of bath plugs. But now, in addition, I had clothing for Dominic, day and nightwear, chosen by Carmel, a pushchair, and umpteen packets of disposable nappies. Those which Dominic didn't need I would leave with the orphanage.

Once through the perfunctory check by Customs, I found my way to the arrivals hall, where Bogdan was waiting for me. We hugged and got straight into his car and drove to his parents apartment.

"They are away for the next few days and the apartment is ours. But first of all, tomorrow, we will go to the British embassy and tie up the remaining details."

"Splendid idea," I said, as we made our way into

Bucharest. The airport, the road and the surroundings had not changed one bit, but my spirits were soaring.

Bogdan looked at me mischievously. "By the way, you should be congratulated."

"Eh? What for?"

"You're a father."

Initially I didn't grasp what he was saying.

"Wake up. The adoption went through on Friday. I've got all the papers at home, and next week we'll have Lily translate them and have them notarised. Dominic's mother has 15 days in which to appeal, if she were to change her mind, but she has already signed a form relinquishing that right. So it's all complete. You have officially adopted Dominic, at least in Romanian law."

I didn't know what to say. To begin with I had intentionally kept Bogdan's endeavours off my radar, because I didn't dare hope that in all the chaos, he would succeed in what effectively was the most logical way out. Latterly, in all the confusion caused by the Department of Health's obduracy, I had actually forgotten about his own endeavours.

"That," I said, "is fantastic. Get out of teeth and get into law!"

"Nah, it was nothing. I picked the mother up from her home, as arranged, we got into court, and it took less than an hour. I'm not sure who was most relieved, me or her."

Dominic was now officially my son. I knew that the UK would not recognise the adoption – Romania was not on the list of recognised countries for the purpose of international adoption – but this was a great step forward.

What I still had to do was to complete adoption proceedings in England. And of course, before that I needed to get him out of Romania.

***

Next morning, at what we judged to be a reasonable hour, we put a call through to the embassy switchboard.

"This is the British embassy," intoned a recorded voice. "Today is a bank holiday in United Kingdom, and the embassy is shut."

I looked at the telephone in exasperation. A bank holiday of all things. I wondered whether Her Britannic Majesty's staff also observed Romanian public holidays, but realised that protest or fury was quite pointless. Nothing could be done and we would have to cool our heels for the next 24 hours.

"Tell you what," said Bogdan, "I need to buy some milk and I have heard that there has been a delivery to Sector 2."

I asked him what he meant. I had already seen that there seemed to be no such things as dairies in the city. Now, as he told me where we were going, I realised that milk was almost impossible to get hold of, and if there was a delivery from a country farm or dairy, word would get around, and families from across the city would rush to the distribution point.

"Come with me in the car and you'll see what I mean."

We drove across the city to an uninspiring area, where we came to crowd of people, some of whom were heading away, carrying what looked like large quart bottles of milk. Bogdan jumped out of the car, telling me to stay put, and he would get hold of some himself. And after a few minutes, he emerged with four of the bottles, placing them carefully on the back seat.

"What are you going to do with them?" I asked. "They are too big to go into your parents' ice box."

"I know. And many of these people you see simply don't have a fridge or ice box anyway."

"So how are they going to keep the milk fresh?"

"They can't, and neither can I, so as soon as we get home, we boil it, and it keeps for longer."

He looked at me. "It's a different world, isn't it? Look at those queues. The one over there is a queue for meat. There is no meat in the shop but they will have heard that a delivery is expected today or tomorrow. It's the same with bread. People queue for yesterday's bread and come away with stale loaves, but it's better than nothing."

He was not trying to be dramatic and clearly wasn't looking for sympathy, but I was profoundly shocked nonetheless that this once-proud nation had been ground down to such a state.

We drove back to the city centre and dropped off the adoption papers with Lily, who promised to have them translated and notarised by Wednesday, before returning to his parents' apartment in silence, trying to work out what to do with the rest of the day.

One thing we had to do. Given the amount of walking I had been doing in the summer heat, I had opted to wear sandals, which were now falling to pieces. One important strap had come away from the sole and the shoe was in danger of disintegrating altogether.

"We'll go to a shoemaker," Bogdan announced.

And within a few blocks of the apartment, he led me to a narrow doorway without any apparent identification and which seemed little different from the photographer's shop which we had visited on our expedition with Dominic. But inside we found two elderly gentlemen surrounded by the usual detritus which is found in cobblers' shops around the world.

I took off my sandal and offered it to one of them, who turned it over, tutting and smiling as he did so. The two of them shared their opinions with Bogdan.

"They're saying that this is rubbish. Look at the workmanship. The strap has come apart because it is only glued to the sole rather than stitched. This would never happen in Romania," he said, grinning. "Shoes are stitched and made of leather, and they last."

I didn't think it would be diplomatic to explain to our cobbler friends that shoes in the UK are invariably not expected, at least in the more fashionable outlets, to last for more than a season, whereupon they would be replaced with something in the current vogue.

I was now without one shoe, but we were assured that repairs would be carried out while we waited, so Bogdan and I sat outside the shop, trying to avoid the dirtier part of the footpath, catching up on our recent endeavours.

We talked about the adoption, his transmission of my faxes to the judge in the law courts, his parents' help and their daily visits to Orphanage Number One.

"You know, one or more of us have been back to that terrible place every day since you left. My parents have managed to get hold of baby food or yoghurt and have tried to tempt Dominic to eat something other than that bottle which he's forced to take."

I didn't deserve their generosity and tried, weakly, to express my gratitude.

"Don't worry. I told you we would succeed. You have been my brother in this and so Dominic is my nephew."

"No," I said, "Dominic will be your godson."

We ducked back in to the shoemakers' den after a respectable wait, and I was handed my newly stitched sandal in exchange for just 30 lei. After offering my profuse thanks, the two of us went back to the apartment, drank coffee and talked some more until eventually it was time for bed.

"Tomorrow, back to the embassy!" he said.

I couldn't wait.

THIRTY

"If someone tells you he is going to make 'a realistic decision', you immediately understand that he has resolved to do something bad."

Mary McCarthy, *On the Contrary*, 1962

Next morning we made our way once more to the embassy, past the harassed police guard, this time to the main consulate door, up steps flanked by reinforced windows. I had to speak through a security flap. Could I speak to Kirsty Rowe? The desk clerk looked doubtful.

"I simply want to confirm that she has received entry clearance from the Home Office," I said. "I won't keep her long, since, as far as I understand it, all the formalities have now been completed."

With obvious reluctance and a good deal of loud buzzes of the kind heard in TV serials featuring American prisons, the main door swung open, and I was allowed in and shown to the Vice Consul's office.

I sat down opposite her, observing her distinct lack of enthusiasm for our meeting.

"I've returned, because I have been assured that the Home Office will have telexed you at the end of last week confirming that entry clearance has been given."

"I'm afraid you're wrong," she said. "We have received a telex but it does not give you permission to enter the United Kingdom."

I was aghast. "That can't be right. I was assured by Mike Lyne that the necessary formalities had been undertaken between the Department of Health and the Home Office, and that Home Office entry clearance was to be transmitted to you immediately."

"I'm sorry," she said, without looking sorry at all, "but I'm telling you what we have received, which is the opposite of what you are suggesting."

"Surely you can contact the Home Office and find out what on earth has gone wrong?"

"I'm not sure that that's our function," she said, "but I'll see what enquiries can be made. I have other things to do, but I suggest that you give me the rest of the day, and ring me at five o'clock this evening, and maybe I'll have some news for you."

I was clearly getting nowhere, so, confused and not a little fed up, I left her and re-joined Bogdan in the hall. We left the building before I dared speak, lest I was heard saying something out of place.

"I don't believe this. Rowe insists that entry clearance has been denied. That simply isn't true, but until this evening, no one is going to contact London and I'm stuck."

"Maybe not. Why don't we ask your lawyer in England to ask what's going on?"

How were we going to do that, I wondered. Then I remembered Tony Coltman's telex machine. "Let's get a telex off to him, and ask him to apply his boot to the Home Office backside."

Bogdan knew immediately where to go. In the middle of the city was a telex office, and in my rucksack was the currency of the day – Kent cigarettes. We sat in his father's car close to a squat building which appeared to be festooned with wires coming out of the roof. There was a crowd of people milling around the entrance, each one intent on shoving their way inside holding a piece of paper carrying a message for transmission abroad.

Bogdan seemed to know what was ahead, and appeared unconcerned by the scene. He found a scrap of paper and together we composed a message, in English, for Tony.

As usual, Bogdan was not at all fazed by the crowd. He fished out a 200 carton of Kent, winked at me, and disappeared.

I wondered how long we would have to wait, given the confusion, but after twenty minutes, he was back, clutching the carbon of the message which had been successfully transmitted.

In the customary upper case lettering which these cumbersome machines utilised, the message read:

'PLEASE TELEPHONE HOME OFFICE IN LONDON, NUMBER 081-686-0333, DEPARTMENT B2, ASK FOR MIKE LYNE OR HIS ASSISTANT. YOU MUST TELL HIM THAT ON THURSDAY 23 AUGUST THE HOME OFFICE TELEPHONED ME AND ASSURED ME AND INSISTED THAT ENTRY CLEARANCE HAD BEEN GIVEN AND A TELEX WAS THAT DAY

TO BE SENT TO BUCHAREST. TODAY, TUESDAY, THE EMBASSY INSIST THAT NO SUCH TELEX OR CLEARANCE HAS BEEN RECEIVED. CAN MR LYNE OR HIS DEPUTY IF HE IS ON LEAVE (I SPOKE TO A MRS MCLUSKEY) PLEASE TELEX AGAIN TO BUCHAREST EMBASSY WITH THE CLEARANCE?'

"I think it's time to get Dominic a passport while we wait. I have a cousin who works in the main passport office. Let's go see him."

Of course, I knew that the orphanage would have been under strict instructions not to release any child until approval had been given by the embassy, and I imagined that the passport office would be subject to the same restriction. I voiced my doubts to Bogdan.

"Remember the window!" said Bogdan. "We'll go and buy some vodka at the dollar shop, and you'll see how quickly this will be sorted out."

We drove to the shop which I'd heard so much about and, sure enough, all sorts of commodities were laid out in a large display which had all the appearance of a cross between a cash-and-carry warehouse and a duty-free outlet. Bogdan used some of my dollars to buy a large bottle of vodka, remembering as he did so to get hold of a paper bag to hide it in. Then on to a nondescript building which he assured me housed the passport office.

Parking the car, he took another carton of Kent and squeezed it into the paper bag with the vodka bottle and, with a cheery wave, disappeared inside the door. I could see myself being drawn further into this unhappy world of black marketing and bribery, but at that moment, bearing in mind the need to get Dominic out and the apparent indifference of both the Romanians and the British to his plight, I felt that I simply had to use every opportunity to get to the front of the queue.

He was out within the hour, with a brand-new Romanian passport, sporting Dominic's photograph and his new name, George Dominic Lissant Cleary. The fact that the passport was, according to Bogdan, endorsed with the caveat that it was for one use only, making it effectively a one-way document, didn't bother me. We were so close to the finishing tape that I felt that I could reach out and touch it.

***

Back at his parent's apartment, I struggled to remain patient. The clock seemed to move agonisingly slowly past 4.30, and then equally slowly towards the time that I should ring the embassy. Bogdan fussed about and turned on the radio, once more tuning into a popular music station.

And once more, there was Elton John wailing about sacrifice.

The minute hand moved slowly.

More echoing words about a baby …

Another minute

… something about different worlds reverberated around the hi-fi …

More seconds passed.

Elton insisting that he was just passing through …

Quite catchy under other circumstances.

The hand moved towards the vertical. I picked up the phone at two minutes to five and dialled the embassy, motioning Bogdan to turn off the radio.

"This is a British embassy," intoned a female voice, "but I'm afraid…"

I interrupted her. "I have been asked by the Vice Consul to telephone her at five o'clock."

"That's not possible, I'm afraid, because, as I was saying, the embassy closes at 5pm."

"That may be so, but I assure you, the Vice Consul made a particular point of asking me to telephone at 5pm." I gave her my name.

The minute hand reached 5pm precisely.

"Look, can I suggest that you speak to the Vice Consul, who I am sure will be prepared to speak to me, since it was she who told to ring at this time."

"I will speak to her and come back to you."

There was a click and the line went silent.

The minute hand passed through one, two and then three minutes past five. Another click, and the telephonist was back on the line.

"I have spoken to the Vice Consul and she is not prepared to speak to you."

"But this is impossible. I rang at the time she told me to."

"I'm sorry but I cannot argue with you. The embassy closes at five and there is nothing more I can do to help you. The office reopens at 10am tomorrow."

"You can tell the Vice Consul, from me that—"

But the line was already dead.

THIRTY ONE

"It is not at all uncommon for someone to arrive at a
scene of brutality or injustice and, with a sympathetic
murmur or heroic flourish, attack the victim. It happens
all the time."

Renata Adler, *Speedboat*, 1977

Wednesday 29th August. Arriving once more,
experiencing that 'air lock' feeling, passing
through the gateway of the British embassy,
leaving the dust and pollution behind us, and walking
through into the fragrant flower beds, trimmed lawns, and
tranquillity of this impossibly fresh oasis – refreshed courtesy
of, as Bogdan remarked, 'Perfidious Albion'. We had decided
to leave our visit until mid morning, in the faint hope that in
the space of 24 hours, the Home Office had been contacted
and had woken up to the problem. Perhaps by now they had
remembered, after all, to telex the entry clearance.

We presented ourselves, again, at the main entrance
where, with obvious reluctance, the security guard buzzed
me through to the entrance hall.

For once, I was not kept waiting long, and Miss Rowe called me into her office.

"Entry clearance has, now, arrived."

"That's a relief. Did it, by chance, come yesterday?"

The Vice Consul looked as if she had just swallowed something unpleasant. "I'm not sure," she muttered.

"You know, as you had asked, I telephoned the embassy at five o'clock yesterday evening, and I was told that you had refused to speak to me."

"Oh," she said dismissively. "There must have been something of a misunderstanding."

"That surprises me. I asked your telephonist to speak directly with you, and I told her that you had spoken to me yesterday morning and had given me the precise time to telephone."

"I don't know anything about that," she said. It was quite clear that I was getting nowhere with a post-mortem, so I let it drop.

"In any event, what is the procedure now?"

"Well, we have been promised entry clearance, so once that comes through formally, I will be in a position to authorise release of the child from the orphanage and you can set in motion the acquisition of a passport."

I said nothing about the passport that we already had, but instead "And how long is that likely to take?"

"It will take several days, and of course we have to be sure that you have the mother's consent, and that the child can be lawfully released from the orphanage. I suggest that you contact me on Friday."

Were it not for the fact that I knew that I had, unknown

to her, already adopted Dominic and that I now had a passport for him, I would have complained bitterly about this further apparent complication, given that every day that he was stuck in Orphanage Number One would be causing him untold damage. However, I kept my peace, and told her that I would return on Friday in the hope that formalities could then be completed.

I imagined that she might well be thinking "don't bank on it", but as far as I was concerned, the final piece of the jigsaw was now in place. Entry clearance was all but secured, and Bogdan and I could start putting in place our exit strategy.

"First things first," I said as soon as we got out of the embassy gates. "Entry clearance is on its way. Why don't we go and get him now?"

"Just what I was thinking. We'll go back to the apartment and pick up his clothes and go straight over to the orphanage."

We picked up his day clothes and a set of nappies and went straight over to Orphanage Number One. The few staff whom we came across recognised Bogdan straight away, and we were allowed through to Dominic's 'pavilion' without difficulty. There, we saw the same doctor who had signed off Dominic's medical report, and Bogdan showed her the adoption papers and the clothes which we had brought. She appeared genuinely pleased and even slightly tearful to hear that we were getting him out, and the general atmosphere in her office took on the character of a mini celebration.

However, we were not allowed to go into the pavilion to collect him. Instead, I watched as one of the orderlies went over and took him out of his cot. Before we could think of dressing him, it seemed pretty obvious that he needed cleaning up. And that particular exercise was again, distressing. She took him over to the stone sink that I had seen when I first went in there and began running the one water tap. She stripped Dominic of the few clothes he was wearing, and lifted him from the cot across to the sink by one arm. Then, dangling him by the same arm, she simply sluiced him down with cold water out of the tap. The whole exercise could only have been more brutal had she dangled him by one leg, the only saving grace being that it was mercifully short, given that he was still such a small child.

She then brought him into the doctor's office, where we dressed him in clothes that neither he nor the staff had ever seen before. Colourful shorts, contrasting little socks and an open neck shirt, a riot of yellows, pinks and emerald green.

Then I picked him up and held my son in my arms.

THIRTY TWO

"We can't form our children on our own concepts; we must take them and love them as God gives them to us."

Goethe, *Hermann and Dorothea*, 1797

Dominic fell ill within hours of his release.

We took him, first, to the park to give him his first taste of freedom and his first sight of greenery. I put him gently on the ground and he staggered slowly up the path, away from us.

"He's just like that singer," joked Bogdan.

"Which singer is that?"

"You know, the one who jerks his arms around and sways in front of the microphone."

"You mean Joe Cocker."

"Absolutely. Look at poor Dom, he can't stand up without swaying about, let alone walk properly. And you know, I guess that he has a touch of rickets, because he's had almost no sunlight through his life, and you can see from the shape of his legs that they haven't been growing entirely normally."

We watched him as he moved around gingerly, taking in, as far as he could, the strange new world to which he had been suddenly introduced.

We didn't want to tire him out, and so we fetched the pushchair and wheeled him around the park for a while before taking him back to the apartment for a rest. I undressed him and put him in a baby-grow and a dry nappy, and then laid him down to rest. Bogdan and I sat next door talking quietly, when suddenly there was a thump from the bedroom.

I hurried in and found Dominic on the floor, looking bewildered. Foolishly, I had forgotten that all the children in the orphanage rocked, some violently, as they lay in their cots, and he was no exception. He had, literally, rocked himself off the bed, and was now lying on the floor, having fallen, probably painfully, but not having made a sound as he hit the floor.

Indeed, he had not made a sound ever since we had taken him from the orphanage, and it was to be some time before he made any sort of pleasurable or distressed sound in his new life.

After packing him securely back on the bed with pillows and cushions on either side of him, we left him to rest a little more, and went back in to see him after an hour. And that was when we noticed that he didn't look well. He was running a high temperature, and his nose was discharging torrents of green mucus. Worse, his neck was swelling up, and his face appeared puffy. After another hour, the glands on his neck had swollen to such an extent that he appeared to be doing a passable impression of a frog.

"I guess that the orphanage has been a barrier to all sorts of common infections," said Bogdan. "He probably hasn't got any immunity against all the things that you and I are breathing in every day."

"But he seems to be in a lot of pain, and he's running a very high temperature. Is there nothing we can do for him?"

"He needs penicillin," said Bogdan. "I think the best thing I can do is to get hold of some and then find a syringe and I will inject him."

Seeing the doubt on my face, he added, "Don't worry. Part of my dental training included administering intravenous drugs and anaesthetics, so I'll not kill him. The only problem we have is getting the right kind of penicillin, and the right size of needle. You stay here with him, and I'll go and see what I can find."

So, while Bogdan went into the city to find medical supplies, I stayed with Dominic, gently rocking him in my arms while he lay, sweating profusely and wriggling from time to time in distress. He was finding it difficult to breathe, and I had to constantly clear the mucus away from his nose.

After a couple of hours, Bogdan returned with something which looked very much like a veterinary syringe and a packet of powder which he assured me could be diluted into a penicillin solution.

He set about his task quietly and efficiently and I shut my eyes while he injected Dominic with his potion. Again, there was no sound from the infant, who now looked even smaller than when I had first found him, and certainly more fragile.

"We still have things to do," said Bogdan, "and we can't carry Dominic round Bucharest while we do them when he is in this state."

I couldn't have agreed more but I wondered what we were going to do to avoid one of us staying in the apartment all day.

"No problem. I have a cousin who has been a midwife. She is retired now, and a widow, and she lives across town, but I am sure that she will care for him while we finish our business."

Not being entirely sure how we would be received, I bundled Dominic up in some blankets, took a supply of nappies and a couple of baby-grows, and we drove across the city in the hope of finding respite for our little boy.

As it turned out, Bogdan's cousin didn't have to be asked twice. A plump middle-aged lady greeted us with a beaming smile, took one look at the overheated scrap of humanity I was holding and swept him up into her arms. Bogdan translated for her.

"She says that it will be absolutely no problem. She will love to look after him for us and she'll feed him up with soup and other goodies, and in a couple of days he will be a different child."

I was so relieved I kissed her, to her great embarrassment, but she again reassured us both in Romanian and shooed us away.

We still had work to do. We needed a visa and we needed to arrange travel back to England and, of course, we had to arrange a flight for three of us. Before I had left for England the first time Bogdan had asked whether I minded allowing him to accompany us. I had reassured him that he needn't have asked – I was intending to ask him that same question.

"Of course you must come to England and you must stay with us, meet Carmel, and come to Dominic's christening, where you will be formally appointed his godfather."

I had remembered the mournful signs outside the British embassy, announcing that no Romanian could visit England without a sponsorship letter and I had remembered to write such a letter in between the telephone calls to the Department of Health while I kicked my heels in England.

"Don't worry about sponsorship," I had said. "I will get the necessary letter to the British embassy so that you can obtain the necessary visa." And that, at least, had worked according to plan, courtesy of the fax machine, and on one of his visits to the embassy, Bogdan had obtained the necessary entry permit.

Things were gradually falling into place. Bogdan had his visa but we still needed formal entry clearance on Dominic's passport and, of course, plane tickets.

We decided to make the embassy our next port of call and we walked back to the now familiar building, through the gate, and to the consulate door. Once again, I asked for the Vice Consul, and once again I was greeted by the impersonal stares of the security personnel at the window.

"Look," I said, "in order to save time, would you be kind enough to give this passport to Miss Rowe and ask her, simply, to endorse it with the necessary clearance or visa so that I can take the child home with me?"

I handed the passport through the grille in the window. The response was electrifying. Within moments, Kirsty Rowe appeared in the doorway. It was quite plain that she was beside herself with anger.

"You have no right to do this," she said, barely controlling herself.

"I don't understand. This is the child's passport and I'm asking you to confirm, on this document, that he has permission to enter the United Kingdom."

"You had no right to get this passport until formal entry clearance had been confirmed by me."

"I hope we're not going through that again," I said. "We both know that entry clearance has been given by the Home Office."

"But you have totally ignored the necessary procedural steps," she insisted.

"I think you'll find that I have not had the greatest of co-operation from your end. But in any event, this discussion is otiose. Last week, I completed the necessary formalities within Romanian law, and I have formally adopted the child. I'm not sure, now, that you can actually stop me travelling to the United Kingdom with him, given my knowledge of the eventual Home Office recognition of my right to entry. It would, however, be of great assistance and avoid complication if you would be kind enough to place the necessary stamp or seal or whatever is needed, on this passport."

Her dissatisfaction was tangible. Without inviting me in, she told me to wait where I was, on the steps of the consulate. Moments later, she returned, and thrust the passport at me.

"I've stamped it," she snapped before turning her back and disappearing back into the building.

I resisted the temptation to thumb my nose in her direction, and instead waved a cheery goodbye to the security clerks at the window, and Bogdan and I walked jauntily out of the grounds.

"Just one thing left," I said. "Tickets."

Still on foot, we found our way to the same Tarom office which I had visited in my attempts to find passage for my mother back to England.

"This is going to be a problem. The last time I came here, there was such a crowd and such a noise that I gave up."

"Ah, yes, but you're forgetting the window thing," Bogdan said, smiling.

And sure enough, no sooner did we get into the smoky and again overcrowded booking hall than he executed a smart right turn and walked through a door set into the wall at one end of the hall, and into a series of offices bisected by a narrow hallway.

Like most Romanians, he had never been allowed to leave the country before then, but he acted as if air travel was second nature to him. Knocking at the doorway of a small cubicle, we found a young woman with perhaps rather too much make-up and rather less than adequate upper clothing, and, smiling broadly at her, Bogdan spoke at length in Romanian.

She made something of a show of deep uncertainty and tried to appear doubtful while she looked at some schedules on her desk, frowning with concentration as she muttered from time to time in response to Bogdan's initial questions.

He turned to me and whispered, "She has told me that all the flights out of Bucharest are booked solid, but that the demand is such that Tarom are thinking of putting an extra flight on this Sunday and if they do, we can have three seats if the necessary arrangements can be made."

He and I knew very well what 'necessary arrangements' meant. He reached into my rucksack and very swiftly passed a 200-cigarette carton of Kent to the young woman, who, with a remarkable sleight of hand, managed to get them out of sight so quickly that despite my proximity to the transfer, I might never have seen it happen.

Her frown disappeared and she smiled at us both. She busied herself with a list which she had found on top of a pile of paperwork on her desk and began scribbling on some sort of manifest while addressing Bogdan, who I realised was giving her our names and Dominic's details.

"She assures me that there will be an extra flight and that we are now booked onto it. She would appreciate it if we paid in dollars."

I was ready for that one and decided not to protest. It was not as if we were being overcharged, but I sensed that the transfer of funds into the airline account would very probably be in lei. Nonetheless, what did I care? As long as Dominic was fit to travel, all the necessary arrangements were now in place.

THIRTY THREE

"And think not you can direct the course of love,
for love, if it finds you worthy, directs your course."

Kahlil Gibran, *The Prophet*

With the help of the young woman at the Tarom office, we managed to secure our three places on the extra flight leaving on Sunday the 2nd September. It had seemed like a lifetime, but in reality the whole expedition, from start to finish, had taken only a little over six weeks. Had I not completed the home study before I set out, it would probably have taken about four months. Nonetheless, I was emotionally exhausted.

We now had a couple of days to kill. Neither of us wanted to sit around the apartment, and we knew that Dominic was being looked after, so Bogdan suggested some sightseeing.

"Really? My only experience looking around Bucharest is that any historical buildings or the like are all boarded up or falling down."

"Which is why we're going out into the country – into the Carpathians."

So off we went, into what Bogdan told me were, in the winter months, snow fields where a rudimentary skiing resort had been constructed. And sure enough, after an hour or so, we pulled up at a ski lift which took us into pleasant rolling hills which, while bearing no comparison to the more sophisticated resorts in the mountains of France and Switzerland, provided a revitalising mixture of fresh air and calm.

Bogdan was clearly pleased that I was experiencing another, rather less filthy, side to my visit. "I'm going to show you a castle. You have heard of Vlad the Impaler?"

In fact I hadn't. Vampires, yes, and dark tales of goings on in the mountains of Moldavia, but nothing about Vlad.

"I've heard of Count Dracula, of course!"

"Maybe," said Bogdan, "but that's all fiction. This guy was real. And not nice. And we'll see his castle."

We drove through a number of villages, some almost medieval in their appearance, thatched roofs falling down, hungry-looking adults and children watching us with empty faces from dark doorways and verandas, until we pulled up at a particularly ugly oil refinery, which appeared to have been dumped for no good reason other than that there was room for it, in spectacular countryside, cheek by jowl with Vlad's castle.

Obviously, Romania had no such thing as a planning policy, or if it did, someone had made, or had been paid to make, a spectacularly horrible decision to allow the monstrosity of the refinery to be built next to the castle of, it was alleged, a monster in his own right.

I shook my head in despair, but joined Bogdan as

we followed a good number of sightseers through the Impaler's apartments and along his battlements, learning as we did so that in common with many medieval rulers, Vlad recognised that brute force was probably the best, if not the only, way to bring a community to order and to protect it against invaders.

"He was not all bad, you see," said Bogdan as he led me through the castle. "He fought off the Ottomans and he rebuilt the economy and made an example of anyone who stood in his way... by impaling them and leaving their bodies in very visible locations, to discourage dissent at home and invasion from abroad."

The name Dracula wasn't, it turned out, an invention – it was hijacked by a Victorian novelist whose name, Bram Stoker, I remembered.

"Vlad's father was 'dracul'," said Bogdan, "which actually means 'dragon'."

As long as we could avoid looking at the huge pipes and funnels of the refinery and ignore the smoke and dirt surrounding the complex, it was not difficult to immerse ourselves in the history of the place, even if we avoided images of torsos and heads stuck on pikes. And I could hardly imagine that the protector of this part of Europe was any more barbaric than the Tudors who were happy enough to hang, draw and quarter their victims in medieval England. And of course I knew that somewhere in Romania, if I had the time to search it out, there would be historical evidence of a civilisation which was certainly as old as England's, fashioned from Roman times and influenced by Eastern migration from the Ottoman Empire, India and beyond.

But we had no time to investigate. We had to collect Dominic, say our goodbyes to Bogdan's parents, and return to England.

***

Another surprise awaited me as we embarked on our flight. We found ourselves on a BAC One-Eleven with English notices and comfortable seats. Bogdan grinned at me.

"You know, your queen gave two or three of these to us."

"Eh?"

"Sure. The evil Ceauşescu was entertained to a state visit to London and the UK government, probably jealous of French influence in our country, thought it would be a good idea to supply three of these jets at a knock-down price. Comfortable, isn't it?"

And, mercifully, it was. The position of the engines was further back down the fuselage, and all we heard was the rushing of air over the wings and round the cabin.

Bogdan and I took it in turns to comfort Dominic on the flight. He was still not in the best shape, and was dreadfully bunged up. However, he slept most of the way to Heathrow and was still asleep as we negotiated our way through immigration. Thankfully, his entry clearance and Bogdan's visa allowed us through without too much difficulty, although we had to spend some time waiting in an ante-room.

True to her word, my mother was waiting for us in a car, which brought a whole new meaning to the word 'compact'. The three of us squeezed in, not an easy task, bearing in mind my mother's size, and we made the journey back to

Warwickshire in reasonable time, without any of us feeling too carsick. Thankfully, my mother's health appeared to have been restored, and she, like us, was delighted to be able to deliver Dominic to his new home.

When we arrived, Carmel met us at the door and swooped on the hot little bundle in my arms. She was quite overwhelmed at the sight of him and disappeared upstairs to clean him up, cool him down, and put him to bed.

And suddenly, it was over.

***

I was home with our son and a new chapter was opening. I had a statutory year to wait, I knew, before I could complete adoption proceedings in England, and I had, of course, to give notice to the local authority of my intention. So, the next day, I telephoned the local office and told them that I had arrived, that Dominic was in one piece, and that in a year's time, I would be starting adoption proceedings.

The woman's voice on the other end of the line was cold.

"What did you call him just now?"

"Dominic."

"But that's not his real name and you cannot call him that."

I felt like responding that I could call him what I liked, but I held my tongue.

"Just make a note, please, that I've returned, that our son is with us, and I will be starting proceedings in 12 months' time. I'm sure you will want to arrange for a social worker to call us, so please let us know and we can make an appointment."

I rang off wondering why it was that we were meeting this level of response, even now. However, as it turned out, we were to be assigned a social worker, Pauline Hope, who could not have been more welcoming, and who delighted in Dominic's progress every time she came to our home.

And that progress was remarkable. In three months, he outgrew three pairs of shoes, size by size, and his growth continued. I had, as David Rapley had asked, taken him to our surgery in the week immediately following our arrival, and he had announced that he was in the very bottom 'centile' of physical development. Six months later, he had progressed almost to the very top.

For the remainder of that year, however, and for the whole of the two years following, he could not talk. No one should be surprised: nobody had spoken to him for more than the first two years of his life.

The back of his head, which had been completely flat when I found him, began to develop a curve and, little by little, he found it easier to walk and climb, although he found the steps up to even the most basic of children's slides to be insurmountable, and I had to lift him up, rung by rung, much to the bemusement of other infants, younger and older, waiting their turns.

Within the month, Dominic was baptised. Family and friends joined us at St Peter's Church in Leamington, and Father Frank Flynn, who was to hold Dominic in a special place in his heart, christened him. Bogdan was, as promised, one of his godparents and he stayed with us, sometimes travelling to London and other parts of the UK, for the next three months, almost as bewildered at the contrast between England and Romania as Dominic.

In the first week that we were back, and perhaps rather thoughtlessly, I took Bogdan shopping to my local Sainsbury's supermarket. As I went about my weekly shop, I noticed that he had lagged behind. I found him in a nearby aisle, confronting a display of rice products. It seemed that the entire presentation extended for half the length of the building, accommodating rice from all parts of Asia, and rice products of every conceivable kind. Even the tinned rice puddings numbered at least half a dozen, some with chocolate, some with cinnamon, and others with fruit and different kinds of cream.

I sensed that he was not simply nonplussed but also quite distressed, remembering, as I did at that moment, his description of the queues in Bucharest which we had left only a week before. There was no way to comfort him.

***

We still had to endure thoughtlessness, sometimes from the most unexpected quarters. When, much later, we introduced him to the nursery reception class of his primary school, the headmistress took Carmel on one side.

"Some of the parents," she said, "are concerned that we satisfy them that Dominic has not got Aids."

While Carmel treated that announcement with contempt, it was still a deeply wounding suggestion. But we were to find, as the years passed, that behaviour of that nature would not be confined to adults who should know better.

We elected to pay for independent, that is, private,

schooling, assuming that the large classes in the state sector would be too difficult for Dominic to cope with. However, any hope that children of families with sufficient means to embark on similar endeavours would somehow not descend to bullying was shattered within a short time of enrolment at school. As years passed, Dominic was subjected to behaviour of which his classmates and their parents should have been ashamed.

And the adoption process itself, which should have concluded with an enjoyable celebration, took place in a way which took me straight back to my experiences in Romania.

The adoption hearing was listed for 10am on the second Monday in September 1991 at Warwick County Court. Carmel, Dominic and I, accompanied by Pauline Hope, attended at the court, in our Sunday best, cameras at the ready, prepared for the celebration hearing. There in good time, we found our way to the court lists and saw our names, but at the appointed time, we were not called. Nor were we called at 10.30, nor 11. Instead, we waited in a large hall, as the end of the morning approached, mingling with the morning's defendants awaiting trial or sentence in the Crown Court.

The crowd of litigants ebbed and flowed around us while we sat, awaiting the pleasure of the judge.

Then, at a little after noon, our names were called and we were ushered into the court of His Honour Judge Gosling, who didn't appear best pleased that his list was being interrupted by an adoption celebration.

We sat down at the side of the court, in the jury seats, while Dominic wandered around the room, pulling papers off the benches in front of him. The judge frowned, looking at the paperwork.

"What is this?" he demanded.

"It's an application to complete the adoption process, and today should be the celebration hearing. Your Honour might note that, in fact, this is the second adoption, because I adopted my son in Romania just over a year ago."

"That's as may be, but the papers in front of me are all in a foreign language."

"No, I think you'll find that every one of them is translated."

The judge paused and shuffled through the papers again.

"But how do I know that the translation is accurate?"

"Because it has been notarised."

"What does that mean?"

Oh, come on. Surely he was just being bloody-minded. How could any lawyer not know? Carmel looked at me enquiringly. Pauline was herself clearly very uncomfortable and fiddled with her camera which was to have recorded this special occasion.

I looked back at the judge. "It means that it has been certified by a Notary Public, an office of which you might have heard."

Another pause while he made heavy weather of understanding the nature of the application, picking up and then discarding the papers in front of him.

Then, "And do I have a social enquiry report?"

"Do you mean from this country or from Romania?"

"I mean from Romania."

"No," I said, "you don't. Nor will you get one, given the

state of social services in that country. You do, however, have all the paperwork from this country and the advice of social services in Warwickshire."

There was another pause. The silence was broken only by the occasional paper or pencil tumbling from the benches in the well of the court as Dominic continued his rounds.

"But…" I finally continued after the silence became even more uncomfortable, feeling both exasperated and concerned that the process was again stalling; perhaps, I thought to myself, I ought to find a different judge, "… I think it is best that I ask you for an adjournment of these proceedings."

More silence. Then, with a sigh, the judge put the papers down.

"Oh, very well," he said, without a trace of humour, "I might as well make the adoption order. There is no need for an adjournment."

And that was that. Pauline was so put out that she completely forgot to take any photographs outside the court building. Neither of us thought it appropriate to ask the judge if he would pose with us inside the court, a tradition which is followed in every adoption celebration hearing throughout the land.

But at least the process was over. Dominic had no idea what had been going on and would be unlikely to remember it. I felt momentarily ashamed of the court process.

I looked around as we emerged from the historic court building. The three of us, finally recognised as a family by English law.

Now it was time to seek out a brother or sister for our son.

POSTSCRIPT

"Confound their politics,
Frustrate their knavish tricks."

Henry Carey, 1693–1743

The information sheet released by the Romanian embassy detailed those orphanages around the country that the authorities were prepared to reveal to the outside world. Ghastly though those institutions were, it is entirely likely that there were more, even more dreadful, which were either too horrible to identify or had simply dropped off the state's radar.

Each of those set out on the sheets released by the embassy had the number of children marked out against each orphanage, in columns. The average appeared to hover around 500–600 children, the same number to be found in Orphanage Number One; and the overall total exceeded six figures, even ignoring those whose identities had been lost.

The vast majority of the children were not orphans at all. Some had been abandoned while others had been passed into state care by parents who were living in absolute poverty and could not provide for them.

The plight of the children had come to international attention when, in 1990, an American news network released the first pictures of an orphanage, accompanying them with a report of what its reporter had discovered.

The Romanian government asserted that urgent attempts would be made to close the orphanages but that, given the scale of the problem, removing the children into foster care or returning them to their families would take a significant amount of time and resources. However, assurances were given to European governments that its ambition to join the Union would be underpinned by a commitment to complete the transition, if not in advance of its accession to the Community, certainly within ten years.

Figures released by the government have revealed the margin by which the target has been missed. Whereas, in 2000, ten years after the revolution, over 57,000 children remained in the orphanages, nearly ten years later, in 2009, UNESCO reported that there were more than 21,000 such children. It is difficult to put an exact figure on the efforts being made to shut down the institutions, since some investigative reports have established that 450 orphanages, accommodating some 160,000 inmates, were shut down by 2007. The contradiction is plain.

Following the introduction of new legislation in Romania in February 1991 concerning adoption, the Romanian government set up the Committee for Adoptions to introduce measures to regularise procedures for the adoption of children, including identifying children who were available for adoption. Adoption of all children by adoptive parents living abroad ceased from 17 July 1991.

The Romanian Committee for Adoptions made it known in November 1991 that further adoption of children by foreign couples would only be permitted where a formal agreement was signed between the Committee and respective countries.

Having continued to refuse to recognise Romanian adoptions, the UK Department of Health finally signed the agreement with the Romanian Committee for Adoptions on 19 March 1992. It was suggested that the Romanian authorities presented their conditions and were prepared to offer little room for manoeuvre. However, it was reported that United Kingdom officials were able to obtain some 'concessions' from the Committee, for example, in the cases of siblings, older children (later defined as children over 10 years of age) or those with special needs, but, in essence, the UK agreement was very similar to those already signed by a number of other countries.

By the spring of 1991, I had felt that Dominic was sufficiently settled to allow me to visit Romania and find him a sibling, but it appeared that the window of opportunity was closing and would be firmly shut by the middle of that year. Finally, on 11 June 1992, following lengthy correspondence, the Parliamentary Under Secretary of State wrote to me, enclosing a copy of the agreement and accompanying guidance. His letter ended:

"You will be disappointed to learn that you do not meet the criteria listed on both age grounds and the number of children in the family."

George Dominic - 8th July 2005

AUTHOR'S NOTE

Bogdan is now married and is in practice as a dentist within shouting distance of New York city. Without his help, I wonder still whether I would have succeeded in my venture. It shouldn't be thought, however, that there was anything particularly special or unique about me or my expedition. At least another one hundred and fifty or so British families undertook the same expedition, both to Romania and Moldavia (as it was then called). Some endured entirely different experiences, suffering obstruction or opposition from one or other or both Countries' authorities. Others found it very simple to find a child, but then had to undertake various subterfuges – and in some cases, outright threats to contact the Press – to get the child back to the UK. I came across a number or entirely good and kind couples who were so overwhelmed with the unpleasantness which they encountered that they felt unable to continue.

A number of months after my return to England with Dominic, the postal services caught up with me and I received a letter from Dr Sadovici. He had finally received my letter some time after I left. He clearly didn't realise that

I was the person whom he had met in Bacau. He wrote to me in studiously polite terms, commending my intentions but warning me against my attempt. I should not think, he wrote, of entering Romania with the intention of removing one or more children, since that would be very much against the children's interests. Had I received his letter before I set off, I wonder, too, whether I might even have thought twice about my endeavour.

Carmel and I were not alone in trying to do something, anything, to ease the suffering of the children in answer to the dreadful newsflashes coming out of Romania. Patrick Crapper, a close family friend begged, badgered and secured supplies and filled a truck loaned by Arnold Laver of Sheffield with nappies, clean laundry, toys and fresh infant clothing and drove from Sheffield to Liverpool where his load joined a convoy to Bucharest in the late Summer of 1990, while Peter Marsh, one of my judicial colleagues, managed to learn and then pass the test to qualify as an HGV driver in six weeks flat, and with the cooperation of the Royal Mail, secured the loan of and drove a post office van with similar supplies from Birmingham to Romania.

Their endeavours and many others have gone unnoticed or have been forgotten. Nonetheless there remain a good number of Church groups who still travel to Romania, having adopted, as it were, particular homes where these unfortunate children still languish. One such group, head-ed up by Jane Williams, regularly travels from Coventry Cathedral.

There are multiple calls on the goodness of the community, all beseeching our charity, and all bewildering the observer with the speed in which they overtake each other in their dreadfulness. I hope that this book will serve as a reminder that Eastern Europe still harbours dark corners where children need help.

As Confucius wrote, it is better to light one small candle than to curse the darkness.

Also from

CRUX
PUBLISHING

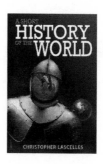

A Short History of the World
by Christopher Lascelles

'A clearly written, remarkably comprehensive guide to the greatest story on Earth - man's journey from the earliest times to the modern day. Highly recommended.'

DAN JONES, author of *The Plantagenets:*
The Kings Who Made England

A Short History of the World is a short and easy-to-read history book that relates the history of our world from the Big Bang to the present day. It assumes no prior knowledge of past events and 32 maps have been especially drawn to give the reader a better understanding of where events occurred.

The book's purpose is not to come up with any ground-breaking new historical theories. Instead it aims to give a broad overview of the key events so that non-historians will feel less embarrassed about their lack of historical knowledge when discussing the past. The result is a history book that is reassuringly epic in scope but refreshingly short in length – an excellent place to start to bring your knowledge of world history up to scratch!